ALAIN LOCKE
REFLECTIONS ON A MODERN RENAISSANCE MAN

ALAIN
LOCKE ᧕‍᪡

REFLECTIONS ON
A MODERN
RENAISSANCE MAN

Edited by Russell J. Linnemann

Louisiana State University
Baton Rouge and London

Designer: Patricia Douglas Crowder
Typeface: Linotron Bembo
Typesetter: G&S Typesetters, Inc.

LIBRARY OF CONGRESS CATALOGING IN PUBLICATION DATA

Main entry under title:
Alain Locke: reflections on a modern Renaissance man.
  "Selected bibliography of the works of Alain Locke": p.
  Includes index.
  Contents: Alain Locke's philosophy of value / Ernest D. Mason—The philosoph-
ical anthropology of Alain Locke / William B. Harvey—Relativism and pluralism in
the social thought of Alain Locke / Rutledge M. Dennis—[etc.]
    1. Locke, Alain LeRoy, 1886–1954—Addresses, essays, lectures.
I. Linnemann, Russell J.
E185.97.L79A64   191   82-7211
ISBN 0-8071-1036-1   AACR2

*For my mother and father
with my heartfelt thanks*

Contents

Preface and Acknowledgments

This book is the outgrowth of a seminar on Alain Locke conducted at Atlanta University from June 12 to August 4, 1978, under the auspices of the National Endowment for the Humanities. The seminar was led by Professor Richard A. Long, director of the Atlanta University Center for African and African American Studies. Those who participated in the session all feel a genuine appreciation for the NEH and believe that its summer program is one of its most useful activities. It succeeds admirably in providing scholars with research opportunities and the chances to enlarge their range of interests which they otherwise would not have.

That the seminar was such a success is a testimony to Professor Long's vast expertise on Locke's life and thought. His suggestions and comments pertaining to research on Locke in particular and Afro-American studies in general were most helpful. He gave freely of his time and pointed toward many fruitful areas of investigation. Much of the credit for what good work came out of the seminar belongs to him.

The librarians at the Trevor Arnett Library of Atlanta University provided vital assistance for the research done there last summer. With unflagging courtesy, competence, and good humor, they rendered yeoman service as they directed participants to, and made available, a variety of archival material, special collections, periodicals, and rare books. Indeed, everyone at Atlanta University went out of his way to make the seminar enjoyable and productive. It was southern academic hospitality at its finest.

I am very indebted to the University of Chattanooga Foundation for its support in the completion of this undertaking. This thoughtful help truly merits my appreciation. I am also deeply grateful for the encouragement and many useful suggestions my wife, Nancy, gave me. Her assistance and patience are sincerely appreciated. Many thanks are also in order for Mrs. Elke Lawson, the History Department secretary who was largely responsible for coordinating the project. Her able efforts at every step of the way smoothed many a path and went far beyond the normal call of duty.

It was a pleasure to work with Catherine Barton, the LSU Press editor whose deft touch vastly improved the manuscript. Very special mention and thanks must also be extended to Rose I. Whitehead. Her tireless efforts as proofreader, indexer, typist, and grandmother made possible the timely completion of the last stages of the project.

Special appreciation is extended to David Graham Du Bois, literary executor of W. E. B. Du Bois, who graciously granted permission to reproduce The Basic American Negro Creed, which appeared in *Dusk of Dawn: An Essay Toward an Autobiography of a Race Concept* (New York: Harcourt Brace, 1940), 320–21.

Introduction

Although Alain Leroy Locke died over one quarter of a century ago in 1954, the passage of time has not dimmed his significance: he remains one of the most important black figures of the twentieth century. A Rhodes scholar, he was a trained philosopher, having done most of his post-graduate study at Oxford, Berlin University, and Harvard, but his areas of expertise ranged far beyond his major field of study. Anthropology, art, music, literature, education, political theory, sociology, and African studies represent only a few of his wide range of intellectual pursuits.

This multiplicity of interests, combined with the fact that Locke was a highly original, productive thinker who left behind a large corpus of published and unpublished work, is, no doubt, the primary reason why a biography of him has not yet been written. A "life and letters" type of effort would be an extremely arduous undertaking, because Locke was not only a prolific critic and essayist but also an inveterate letter writer who seemingly knew everyone and corresponded with each of them at one time or another.

By the same token, an "intellectual biography" would probably prove to be an even more herculean task, given his erudition in so many different academic areas. Locke was no dilettante; he was an incisive, fertile, creative thinker who made significant contributions to each of the modes of thought that came under his scrutiny. Consequently, few if any potential biographers who might wish to examine the scope of his thought, assess his often provocative contributions, and place them within the context of the appropriate disciplines, would have the intellectual breadth or depth to fulfill the task properly.

Clearly, there is a crying need in Afro-American studies for this lacuna to be filled. On an irregular basis articles about Locke have appeared in scholarly journals, but since his death in 1954, there have been few useful ones. Authors almost always try to fit him into a racial context, and seldom, if ever, do any of them attempt to look beyond the color implications of his conceptions. The consequence of this is that there is neither a compilation of articles or essays on Locke which would be useful to scholars, nor is there a compendium of his thought. Therefore, those who are interested in the man and his ideas and who are not fortunate enough to be near a major library generally must search painstakingly for difficult-to-obtain older journals, various reprint series, or microfilmed special collections.

Unfortunately, most of what little has been written about Locke in the last twenty-five years is mainly concerned with his activities surrounding the Harlem Renaissance. He is widely recognized as a pivotal figure in the movement; his book *The New Negro*, which was published in 1925, is perhaps his best-known work. Not only did he popularize the description of the period, he was primarily the individual who defined it. His contribution to the movement did not end there. His advice was frequently sought and he acted as a cultural facilitator, indefatigably giving encouragement, assistance, and support to a great number of literary and other cultural figures whose accomplishments constitute the heart of the renaissance.

To a much lesser but still very important degree, attention has been devoted to Locke's views on art. He was among the first major black American critics and commentators on African and Afro-American art. Indeed, one of his most significant publications, *The Negro and His Art*, deals with this topic. Art came to hold a lifelong fascination for Locke. Not only did he become a collector, he also played a lion's role in establishing and expanding the art gallery at Howard University, where he taught for approximately forty years. Throughout his adult life, he constantly urged the systematic study of African art, not solely for artistic reasons but for cultural, philosophical, and sociological ones as well.

The other area of Locke's thought with which the layman might have come into contact would be his comments on literature. For years he wrote retrospective reviews of black literature which appeared in such periodicals as *Phylon* and *Opportunity*. These essays on black literature, coupled with a set of highly developed philosophical values he penetratingly applied to them, cemented his reputation as a literary critic of considerable magnitude. Many authors, both established and aspiring, sent their work to him for his opinions or suggestions, and he was frequently asked to write forewords for a wide variety of books.

Certainly the explosion of interest in black studies in this country over the last twenty-five years accounts in good measure for the interest in Locke's observations about these topics. Laymen and scholars alike have been deeply concerned with the search for a black identity, the formulation of a black aesthetic, and an elaboration of the black cultural experience. Naturally, there was a rekindled interest in black art and literature (whether found in Africa or in the diaspora) as well as the desire to explore anew the cultural dimensions and aesthetic implications of the Harlem Renaissance. Thus, it is apparent that contemporary issues and concerns which revolved around race greatly determined which aspects of his work would receive significant scholarly attention.

While it is only natural and commendable that those interested in black art, literature, and the Harlem Renaissance should turn to Locke, many other dimensions of his thought, particularly on music, philosophy, and education, had relevance not only for the immediate, burning cultural issues of the 1960s but for broader questions dealing with aesthetics, racial relations, and politics as well. Also, various avenues of Locke's concerns, most notably in certain aspects of his anthropological and philosophic thought, transcend the question of race entirely. Lamentably, they have been largely untouched even by recent scholarship.

This collection of essays endeavors to focus on topics in Lockean thought that, for one reason or another, have not yet received the attention they deserve. Obviously, no respectable work devoted to this great thinker could ignore his contributions to art and literature or his ties to the Harlem Renaissance, but these essays do not seek to emphasize them to the exclusion of everything else. Specifically, special regard will be given his philosophical and anthropological concepts. He was deeply involved with anthropology in general and questions of cultural pluralism in particular, and some of the more salient aspects of his thought will be examined here. It might well surprise some who know little of Locke's anthropological theories to discover just how useful and timely they are to the contemporary world.

Similarly, even though Locke was engaged in education for all of his adult years, wrote extensively and incisively about music, stood out as a pioneer of African studies, and was extremely interested in the impact political questions had on black people, little is generally known about his positions on these topics, and there is virtually no good, recent comment or exegetical criticism of them. Of course, this collection is no substitution for a compendium of his scholarly output, but it can provide a sense of the depth and breadth of his multidisciplinary vision and interests while at the same time amplifying key aspects of his conceptual framework.

Even though there is a tremendously broad range of subject matter covered herein, Locke's profound system of philosophy, especially in the realms of values, aesthetics, and pluralism, gives a general sense of cohesiveness to the collection. Despite his sundry interests, Locke always remained a true philosopher at heart. Consequently, there is an inherent sense of consistency in most of his thought, even though his ideas were frequently compartmentalized in different disciplines.

In many ways, Locke never outgrew or discarded the major philosophical positions he staked out as a promising graduate student. As he matured intellectually, he refined his arguments, but his essential assertions about value theory, aesthetics, culture, and pluralism remained relatively constant. Therefore, when one steps back and tries to bring the quintessential Locke into focus, there is a remarkable sense of unity to the composite body of his thought, both in a temporal and in a multidisciplinary sense. The selections in this volume are designed to give the reader a perception of Locke's consistent vision and some insight into the way in which he tried to render intelligible and harmonious an often contradictory, hostile world. When the view of Locke that is contained in these selections is combined with popular perceptions of him, a much more accurate portrait of the man should develop. It is hoped that this volume will rekindle an appreciation for his many contributions and will serve as an impetus to a sorely needed renaissance in Lockean studies.

ALAIN LOCKE

REFLECTIONS ON A MODERN RENAISSANCE MAN

Alain Locke's Philosophy of Value

ERNEST D. MASON

Contemporary opinions of Alain Locke's philosophical stature vary enormously. In some quarters he is dismissed as having been no philosopher at all, only an acute literary and social critic. Locke himself seemed to suggest this attitude when he described himself as "more of a philosophical mid-wife to a generation of younger Negro poets, writers, and artists than a professional philosopher."[1] Numerous others, however, regard Locke as one of the most important philosophical thinkers of his day. The American philosophers Sidney Hook and Horace M. Kallen thought Locke important enough to include his essay, "Values and Imperatives," in their anthology, *American Philosophy, Today and Tomorrow*; Edgar S. Brightman, in his *An Introduction to Philosophy*, thought him important enough to quote him on the nature of value theory; and the professional philosophers who organized the yearly Conference on Science, Philosophy and Religion—John Dewey, Roy Wood Seellers, F. S. C. Northrop, and Richard McKeon to mention only a few—thought him important enough to include several of his philosophical articles in their publications. For these reasons alone, it

1. From the self-portrait that accompanies Locke's essay, "Values and Imperatives," in Horace Meyer Kallen and Sidney Hook (eds.), *American Philosophy, Today and Tomorrow* (New York: Lee Furman, 1935), 312.

I

seems that the former estimation (including Locke's own assessment) greatly underrates Locke as a genuine philosophical thinker. True, Locke needed to devote more time and effort in his later life to the development of the philosophical ideas contained in his early writings to be considered one of the world's "great" philosophers. But the provocative and interesting philosophical suggestions he did make, along with his serious efforts at their elaboration, constituted a highly significant accomplishment, amply justifying the designation of him as one of the important philosophical thinkers of his era.

There is no need here to trace at length the historical development of axiology or value theory; but to place Locke in some historical perspective we should at least mention a few significant names and themes.[2] Modern value theory has its origin as a philosophic discipline in the attempts of certain philosophers to discover a common core of valuation as it occurs in its wide variety of settings: ethics, economics, aesthetics, religion, political science, jurisprudence, etc. Initiated in the second half of the nineteenth century by the German, Hermann Lotz, and the Austrians, Franz Brentano, Alexius von Meinong, and Christian von Ehrenfels, value theory made remarkable strides in Central Europe, France, Italy, Spain, and America. While Plato, Aristotle, and other early philosophers who investigated the domains of ethics, aesthetics, economics, religion, and politics dealt with values *factually*, they did so without realizing that such qualities as goodness, beauty, and utility have certain features in common that could be studied in a specific discipline. It is that discipline which today is called axiology, philosophy of values, or value theory. To use the definition of the American philosopher, Ralph Barton Perry, the philosophy of values may thus be defined as "that branch of knowledge in which such sciences as theory of knowledge, ethics, political science and jurisprudence, economics, aesthetics and philosophy of religion are unified and distinguished. It would be the task of such a theory of value

---

2. For an excellent statement on the origin and nature of axiology, see Stephen C. Pepper, "A Brief History of General Theory of Value," in Vergilius Ferm (ed.), *A History of Philosophical Systems* (New York: Philosophical Library), 394–503.

first to bring to light the underlying principle common to these sciences, and then to employ this principle for the purpose of arbitrating between them."[3]

Locke, whose dissertation was done under the directorship of Perry at Harvard, was profoundly influenced by his teacher's conception of a general theory of value. He was especially convinced of Perry's notion that one of the most important functions of value theory is to provide a rational ground for the comparison of values, particularly those ultimate values by which men estimate their civilization, their progress, and the salvation of their existence. Thus viewed, the problem of values constitutes the very core of human life and, as Locke points out in his review of Perry's *Realms of Value* (1954), is

> one of the most important and most baffling of the provinces of philosophy. Its importance as a primary point of contact between thought and actual living is seldom given proper emphasis in either professional or lay thinking. The reasons are many, among them our chronic inclination to take values for granted. . . . It is both a notable and welcome exception to encounter an analysis of value that, without loss of scholarly depth, examines values in the vital context of their actual functioning, and as in the case of *Realms of Value*, yields cumulative insight into the role of values in motivating and in providing sanctions—rational and rationalized—for our civilization.[4]

Written in 1954, the year of Locke's death, this statement clearly reveals his belief in the importance of values in human affairs. But precisely what, we may ask, are values for Locke and how do they affect our daily life? To answer this, we must first turn to Locke's analysis of the problem, in his dissertation.

Feeling as the Basis of Value

Locke's dissertation, "The Problem of Classification in the Theory of Value, or an Outline of a Genetic System of Values," is his most thorough statement on the problem of value. It was written largely

3. Ralph Barton Perry, *General Theory of Value* (New York: Longmans, Green, 1926), 9.

4. Alain Locke, "Values that Matter," *Key Reporter*, XIX (May, 1954), 4.

under the influence of the American philosopher, Wilbur Marshall Urban, and a number of German and Austrian value theorists, notably, Brentano (1838– 1917), Von Meinong (1853–1920), and Von Ehrenfels (1859– 1932). In examining the dissertation, our goal will not be to exhaust it completely but simply to make explicit the basic problems and ideas that are necessary for understanding Locke's subsequent thinking.

As the title indicates, Locke is interested here in the rather abstract and technical problem of classification in value theory. In method Locke's approach to this problem is phenomenological and genetic. Phenomenologically, it attempts to explore and describe the psychological phenomena of valuational experiences; genetically, it traces the origin and development of these experiences in terms of the psychological processes involved. The essence of his position is that values should be classified in terms of the psychological or affective factors involved in the valuational experience. As Locke himself states it, "Our views . . . are that value kinds or types represent for the most part psychologically differentiated modes of valuation and that appropriate principles and units for value classification can only issue from a general theory of value which succeeds in proving that affective factors discoverable and psychologically operative in the primary process of valuation are determinative of value type."[5]

By "value kinds or types" Locke has in mind the quality or essential nature of the value in question, that is, whether or not a value is constructed to be ethical, aesthetic, religious, economic, etc. To explain further how a particular value comes to be understood in one way as opposed to another, Locke relies on the ideas of Wilbur Marshall Urban. What is of most interest to Locke is Urban's notion of "value-movements," an expression that refers to the specific way in which values are actually sensed and felt. Basically there are two possible kinds of value-movements, two possible ways of sensing and feeling: those toward what Urban calls the

5. Alain Locke, "The Problem of Classification in the Theory of Value" (Ph.D. dissertation, Harvard University, 1918), 1–2.

"transgredient reference" and those toward the "immanental reference." The transgredient reference is characterized by the sensing or feeling of tension and restlessness as exemplified in the ethical attitudes of obligation, honesty, or justice. The immanental reference, in contrast, is characterized by relaxation and quiescence, features that are generally characteristic of aesthetic valuations and feelings. To rid ourselves of cumbersome terms and avoid confusion, we shall hereafter refer to these two basic ways of sensing and feeling values as the ethical and aesthetic attitudes respectively. It is, according to Locke, upon these two attitudes that the various other values—economic, religious, logical, and hedonic—are conditioned.

One of the more interesting and original features of Locke's theory of value is his attempt to demonstrate that the various kinds of values, especially the ethical and aesthetic, are interchangeable. Though initially discussed in his dissertation, the idea of value conversion, mergings, and opposition finds its best expression in his essay "Values and Imperatives" (1935). Here Locke points out how logical reasoning sometimes takes on the aesthetic character of a "beautiful proof" or a "pretty demonstration," or how a religious ritual may only be an aesthetic or symbolic show to the noncredal spectator but a genuine mystical "reality" to the convinced believer. These and similar observations lead Locke to infer that the identity of values as a group or class necessarily rests on other elements, namely, feelings and attitudes. "We know," says Locke, "a *value genre* often evades its definition and breaks through its logical barriers to include content not usually associated with it. The awe-inspiring scene becomes '*holy*,' the logical proof, '*beautiful*,' creative expression, a '*duty*.'" In each instance, the new predicate follows a certain specific attitude that cancels out the traditionally employed predicate. What this means for Locke is that "for every value coupled by judgemental predication, thousands are linked by identities of feelings-mode; for every value transformed by change of logical presuppositions, scores are switched by a radical transformation of the feeling attitude. We are forced to conclude that the feeling-quality, irrespective of content, makes a value of a given kind, and that a transformation of the attitude effects a change of type in the value situation."[6]

Values, then, have their origin in a specific feeling or attitude toward an object. The conclusion to be drawn from this psychological analysis of the original apprehension of values is briefly summarized by Locke:

> If values are thus normatively stamped by form-qualities of feeling in the original value experience, then the evaluative judgement merely renders explicit what was implicit in the original value sensing, at least as far as the moral quality of the value is concerned. This could only be true on one of two assumptions, *viz.*, that some abstract feeling-character functioned dispositionally as a substitute for formal judgement, or that the feeling-attitude itself moulded the value-mode and reflected sympathetically its own pattern. If the latter be the case, a value-type or category is a feeling-mode carved out dispositionally by a fundamental attitude.[7]

The distinction between the evaluational experience and the act of evaluation, or between *the original value experience* and the *evaluation* of that experience constitutes the core of Locke's theory of value. The original value sensing is always a direct and immediate experience, and like all direct and immediate experiences, it is supposedly noncognitive. An evaluative judgment, on the other hand, is clearly an intellectual act that attempts to *examine* our original value experience to determine its worth. What this means for Locke is simply that the existence of end-values is not necessarily mediated by a process of evaluation or by a formal, logical value judgment. Instead, certain basic feeling-attitudes normally condition these end-values prior to the intellectual act of formal evaluation. Men, says Locke, are indeed rational, but they are first of all emotional.

Hence to point out the dependence of logical or rational thought

6. Locke, "Values and Imperatives," 321.
7. *Ibid.*, 320.

on feelings is the basic intent of Locke's distinction between the original value sensing and the evaluation of that affective sensing. One of the most important consequences of the failure to recognize this complex psychological process is a mistaken notion of *facts*—the notion that they are simple, pure, neutral things, easily defined and explained. For Locke such an idea is a mere abstract mental construction, stemming largely from an almost religious faith in the methods of modern science. All data, all experiences, scientific or otherwise, occur within a context, a context that necessarily includes for the experiencing or evaluating subject an elaborate network of concepts, models, and associations that are cultural and normative in function and pervaded by feeling and emotion. What everything adds up to is the impossibility of conceiving any kind of pure fact or independent reality. "Facts" or "reality" are merely what people interpret them to be, and as different people have different conceptions of them, it follows that they both must be conditioned by other, external factors.

Despite its apparent soundness, however, Locke realized that such an extreme relativistic conception of human thinking and valuing could not win in a walkover. That is, not only was relativism forced to confront itself on logical contradictions and consequences, it had to defend itself against such equally attractive views as value absolutism and value monism.

The Nature of Locke's Value Relativism

Locke's decision to refer to his philosophy of value as "value relativism" raises a number of difficulties, most of which stem from his failure to define the expression with any great precision. At times it seems to be synonymous with "value pluralism," at other times with "value subjectivism." The real problem arises when relativism is confused with the latter, subjectivism. According to the subjectivist, the values I cherish are good for me and the ones you cherish are good for you. Value judgments are neither objectively true nor objectively false, but merely the expression of personal attitudes, needs, interests, and tastes masquerading as rational judgments.

The seriousness of this doctrine lies in its denial of the existence of any objective standard that would enable us to distinguish "right" from "wrong." In pointing out that "values are rooted in attitudes, not in reality and pertain to ourselves, not the world," Locke seems to be supporting such an extreme relativism.[8]

But elsewhere in "Values and Imperatives," Locke attacks the doctrine of subjectivism, referring to it as "Protagorean relativism,—each man the measure and the gauge of value." However— and this is where the difficulty enters—not only is Locke critical of this form of extreme subjectivism, he is equally critical of the so-called truths of science that are said to be valid for all situations, all men, and all times. "What seems most needed," he says, is "some middle ground between these extremes of subjectivism and objectivism. The natural distinction of values and their functional criteria surely lie somewhere in between the atomistic relativism of a pleasure-pain scale and the colorless, uniformitarian criterion of logic."[9]

The difficulty of stating his position without lapsing into subjectivism on the one hand and complete objectivism on the other leads Locke to the observation that "the gravest problem of contemporary philosophy is how to ground some normative principle or criterion of objective validity for values without resort to dogmatism and absolutism on the intellectual plane, and without falling into their corollaries, on the plane of social behavior and action, of intolerance and mass coercion."[10] Thus formulated, it appears that what Locke is really trying to solve is not so much the epistemological problem of subjectivism versus objectivism, but the very practical, political, and social problem of *value absolutism* and *value dogmatism*. The question now becomes, in trying to determine objective standards for the evaluation of values, how do we avoid dogmatism and absolutism, claims of finality, intolerance, and forced conformity?

To demonstrate how Locke attempted to solve this difficulty, we

8. *Ibid.*, 328.
9. *Ibid.*, 319.
10. *Ibid.*, 315–16.

must first place the statement most responsible for the confusion, that values are "rooted in attitudes, not in reality," in its proper context. Before making this remark, Locke spoke of Nicolai Hartmann's observation that values have a tendency to overpower the individuals who hold them and establish themselves as absolutes at the expense of others. As Hartmann has well observed: "Every value, when once it has gained power over a person, has a tendency to set itself up as a sole tyrant of the whole human *ethos*, and indeed at the expense of other values, even of such as are not inherently opposed to it. We must acknowledge this, though not to despair over it, but by understanding how and why, to find principles of control from the mechanisms of valuation themselves." It is at this point that Locke says: "The effective antidote to value absolutism lies in a systematic and realistic demonstration that values are rooted in attitudes, not in reality and pertain to ourselves, not to the world. Consistent value pluralism might eventually make possible a value loyalty not necessarily founded on value bigotry, and impose a truce of imperatives . . . by insisting upon the reciprocity of these norms."[11]

Here it becomes clear that Locke evokes the principle of value relativism primarily as an antidote to value absolutism, which, for Locke, is just one step away from political absolutism. For by presenting values as transcendent, absolute entities, independent of individuals, absolutism makes it impossible for a person to say what he considers to be of value. He can only bow to these absolute values which are somehow "out there." In citing Hartmann as an example of absolutism in values, Locke did not do so arbitrarily. When Nicolai Hartmann propounded this theory of values in his *Ethik* (1926), the Nazi party was engaged in a desperate fight for the conquest of political power over Germany. Whether Hartmann wanted it or not, he could not prevent the intellectuals among the Nazis from using his theory of values to propagate the cause of Hitlerism among the German intelligentsia. With Hartmann's the-

11. *Ibid.*, 328.

ory it was now understood that the new values proclaimed by the Führer were not just the inventions of a cruel, perverse demagogue who appealed to the lowest instinct of the masses, but eternal, absolute essences that everybody had to accept. The Führer had merely discovered these absolutes and was only trying to direct his people towards them.

Though critical of value absolutism, Locke was, as noted, equally critical of the dangers of value relativism—of the chaos of values opposed to each other, without any possibility of deciding which of them was right and which of them was wrong. To use Locke's own formulation of the problem: "At the same time that it takes sides against the old absolutism and invalidates the *summum bonum* principle, this type of value pluralism does not invite the chaos of value-anarchy or the complete *laissez faire* of extreme value individualism." [12]

The attempt to solve this difficult issue led Locke to the conclusion that to do justice fully to the wide range and variety of human values they must be studied in their historical, social, and cultural context. It is at this point that Locke's philosophy of value abandons its strictly psychological approach, with its emphasis on the isolated individual, for a more detailed consideration of the external determinants of value. For just as values and norms are primarily based on feelings and attitudes, feelings and attitudes have their own determinants. For Locke these determinants or conditioners are history, society, and culture.

The sociohistorical approach to the problem of value receives a great deal of attention in one of Locke's earliest writings, "The Concept of Race as Applied to Social Culture" (1924). He proposes in this essay the following method as a more accurate procedure for understanding cultural values: "first, its analytic and complete description in terms of its own culture-elements, second its organic interpretation in terms of its own intrinsic values as a vital mode of living, combined if possible with an historical account of its devel-

12. *Ibid.*, 328–29.

opment and derivation." By "intrinsic value," Locke has in mind those vital, functional value norms that sustain a particular culture's identity and existence, or its "vital mode of living." This involves, basically, the manner in which a culture structures reality or the things of nature in order to make sense of the world. It involves, in short, understanding man socially and culturally; Locke calls it the "principle of organic interpretation." So not only should we recognize that values are plural, we must undertake a functional and historical interpretation of values in order to gain some understanding of their validity or appropriateness in the context in which they are employed, or in the total context of a "mode of living." This is Locke's way of pointing out that there is only a "relative and functional rightness, with no throne of absolute sovereignty in dispute."[13]

In what is for our purpose a more important essay written some twenty-six years later, Locke refers to this method of understanding values as "critical relativism."

Carried through as a consistent methodological approach, critical relativism would

1. implement an objective interpretation of values by referring them realistically to their social and cultural backgrounds,

2. interpret values concretely as functional adaptations to these backgrounds, and thus make clear their historical and functional relativity. An objective criterion of functional sufficiency and insufficiency would thereby be set up as a pragmatic test of value adequacy or inadequacy,

3. claim or impute no validity for values beyond this relativistic framework, and so counteract value dogmatism based on regarding them as universals good and true for all times and all places,

4. confine its consideration of ideology to the prime function and real status of being the adjunct rationalization of values and value interests,

13. Alain Locke, "The Concept of Race as Applied to Social Culture," *Howard Review*, I (June, 1924), 299; Alain Locke, "Pluralism and Intellectual Democracy," in *Second Symposium* (New York: Conference on Science, Philosophy, and Religion, 1942), 200.

5. trace value development and change as a dynamic process instead of in terms of unrealistic analytic categories, and so eliminating the traditional illusions produced by generalized value terms—viz., static values and fixed value concepts and "ideals,"

6. reinforce current semantic criticism of academic value controversy by stressing this realistic value dynamic as a substitute for traditional value analytics, with its unrealistic symbols and overgeneralized concepts.[14]

The shift in emphasis from the psychological to the historical, social, and cultural in comprehending values makes clear the dependence of Locke's social and cultural philosophy on his philosophy of values. The shift also indicates that the primary intent of his value theory is essentially ethical. It is ethical, that is, insofar as it demands that we treat people different from ourselves with respect, with concern, and above all with understanding and tolerance. Undoubtedly, the major obstacle we must overcome before achieving this type of outlook is the belief that before people of different races and cultures can live togther they must adhere to the same principles and values. In his article "Unity Through Diversity: A Baha'i Principle" (1930), Locke takes issue with this view, arguing that "spiritual unity is never achieved by an exacting demand for conformity or through any program of imposed agreement. In fact, the demands of such an attitude are self-defeating. What we need to learn most is how to discover unity and spiritual equivalence underneath the differences which at present so disunite and sunder us, and how to establish some basic spiritual reciprocity on the principle of unity in diversity." Realizing that individuals will continue to cherish the values of their society, culture, race, or nation, Locke goes on to point out elsewhere that "it should be possible to maintain some norms as functional and native to the process of experience, without justifying arbitrary absolutes, and to uphold some categoricals without calling down fire from heaven. Norms of this

14. Alain Locke, "The Need for a New Organon in Education," in *Goals for American Education* (New York: Ninth Symposium of the Conference on Science, Philosophy, and Religion, 1950), 209–10.

status would be functional constants and practical sustaining imperatives of their correlated modes of experience; nothing more, but also nothing less." [15]

The best way to keep our imperatives in bound then is to realize that our ends represent only one aspect of human experience and that they stand only for a subsistent order of reality. We should not confuse them with complete objective reality or endow them with universality, for as imperatives of behavior and action, they are purely functional and relative. To use Locke's own metaphor, we should "think of reality as a central fact and a white light broken up by the prism of human nature into a spectrum of values. . . . As derivative aspects of the same basic reality, value orders cannot reasonably become competitive and rival realities." Given this pluriverse of values, Locke thinks that the best thing to do is to follow Josiah Royce's principle of "loyalty to loyalty": "It is the Roycean principle of 'loyalty to loyalty,' which though idealistic in origin and defense, was a radical break with the tradition of absolutism. . . . In its larger outlines and implications it proclaimed a relativism of values and a principle of reciprocity. Loyalty to loyalty transposed to all fundamental value orders would then have meant, reverence for reverence, tolerance between moral systems, reciprocity in art, and had so good a metaphysician been able to conceive it, relativism in philosophy." Peaceful coexistence thus hinges upon the individual's ability to cherish his values sensibly and practically, which means consciously avoiding dogma, bigotry, and arbitrary orthodoxy. In an excellent summary of his position, Locke says:

In the pluralistic frame of reference value dogmatism is outlawed . . . value profession or adherence on that basis would need to be critical and selective and tentative (in the sense that science is tentative) and revisionist in procedure rather than dogmatic, final and *en bloc*. One can visualize the difference by saying that with the many articles of faith, each article would need independent

15. Alain Locke, "Unity Through Diversity: A Baha'i Principle," *Baha'i World*, IV (1930), 373; Locke, "Values and Imperatives," 329.

scrutiny and justification and would stand, fall or be revised, be accepted, rejected or qualified accordingly. Fundamentalism or the 'all or none' or 'this goes with it' varieties could neither be demanded, expected nor tolerated. Value assertion would thus be a tolerant assertion of preference, not an intolerant insistence on agreement or finality. Value disciplines would take on the tentative and revisionist procedure of natural science.[16]

After years of racism, segregation, lynchings, and international and cultural conflicts, Locke, who as we noted once minimized the importance of logic and the scientific attitude, is now thoroughly convinced of the need to supplement our original value feelings with deadly serious, critical reflections.

Men, History, Values, and Imperatives

It is beyond dispute that the emergence and decay of cultural epochs in the course of human history are reflected in man's shifting valuations; that his response to his social environment and to the world as a whole are value oriented; that, in fact, man's entire life is dominated by values and value conflicts. As Locke states it,

The common man, in both his individual and group behavior, perpetuates the problem in a very practical way. He sets up personal and private and group norms as standards and principles, and rightly or wrongly hypostasizes them as universals for all conditions, all times and all men. Whether then on the plane of reason or that of action, whether 'above the battle' in the conflict of 'isms' and 'the bloodless ballet of ideas' or in the battle of partisans with their conflicting and irreconcilable ways of life, the same essential strife goes on, and goes on in the name of eternal ends and defined ultimates.

Though convinced that such "defined ultimates" always pose a threat to life, Locke is quick to add that "in de-throning our absolutes, we must take care not to exile our imperatives, for after all, we live by them. We must realize more fully that values create these

16. Locke, "Values and Imperatives," 332; Alain Locke, "Cultural Relativism and Ideological Peace," in *Approaches to World Peace* (New York: Fourth Symposium of the Conference on Science, Philosophy, and Religion, 1944), 610.

imperatives as well as the more formally super-imposed absolutes, and that norms control our behavior as well as guide our reasoning."[17] The hierarchy of things and ideas conceived by men are thus intimately linked with the imperative for action; and to avoid one's actions being thwarted by another, men and groups of men try to impose upon others the hierarchies in which they believe. It is from this forced loyalty that most of the ideological, political, and cultural conflicts that characterize human history have their origin. But as our consideration of Locke's value theory demonstrates, he never ceased asking: Is there any possible way of deciding the validity of these conflicting claims and of establishing a unitary principle of rightness and wrongness of values, apart, that is, from their function within a particular historical, social, or cultural context? Although unable to solve this problem philosophically, Locke was able in his own practical life and thinking to cherish certain conceptions of "right" and "wrong" without, as he says, "calling down fire from heaven."

The solution consists, on the one hand, of assigning a positive value to any effort aimed at overcoming conflicts in human relations due to opposing values and, on the other, of assigning a negative value to any effort aimed at erecting stronger barriers between people of different interests and desires. The measure in which an effort approaches the aim of removing such barriers between human beings determines for Locke the *degree* of its positive or negative value. Peaceful coexistence should thus be construed here neither as an absolute imperative nor as a transhistorical value, but merely as a principle, philosophic or social, which serves as a criterion for assessing the positive or negative character of values.

The idea of living together peacefully is, of course, central in the history of Western political, social, and ethical thought. But what makes Locke's approach to the problem so refreshing is his emphasis on the element of "feeling" in our political, social, and ethical life, an emphasis which makes it possible for Locke to make much

17. Locke, "Values and Imperatives," 313–14, 315.

better sense of human intolerance and conflict than most single-minded, "rational" intellectuals. If we follow Locke's thinking, we learn that it is not a deficiency of thought or knowledge that prevents people from living together, but a deficiency of *feeling*. Our feelings dictate our absolutes; other people do not matter. The "taproot" of these feelings stems, says Locke, "more from the will to power than from the will to know. Little can be done, it would appear, either toward their explanation or reconciliation on the rational plane. Perhaps this is the truth that Brentano came near laying hands on when he suggested a love-hate dimensionality as fundamental to all valuation. . . . The role of feeling can never be understood nor controlled through minimizing it; to admit it is the beginning of practical wisdom in such matters."[18]

Locke's philosophy of value is not, however, a philosophy of feeling; it merely recognizes that feeling has its place in the total texture of human existence. He believes that if we reflect on our own nature, if we attend to our own neglected outlying motives, feelings, and attitudes, we shall be in a better position to judge and understand not only ourselves but others as well. What ultimately rules us is neither history, culture, nor society, but our own emotional nature, our own imperatives. Hence with self-reflection and self-scrutiny, we are in a much better position to tame the "wild forces" of these imperatives and to achieve that genuine coexistence for which Alain Locke so passionately, thoughtfully, and humanely lived.

18. *Ibid.*, 328.

The Philosophical Anthropology of Alain Locke

WILLIAM B. HARVEY

In the tradition of Renaissance figures, Alain Locke applied his considerable intellectual talents to a wide variety of scholarly and artistic pursuits. Though his formal academic background and training was in philosophy, Locke was also a knowledgeable person in the fields of literature, music, art, psychology, and the physical sciences.[1] Certainly, ample documentation of Locke's multifaceted intellectual character has been provided; history has recorded both his accomplishments and the plaudits of his colleagues and comrades. The breadth and depth of his writings show Locke to be not simply a contributor but an original thinker in several of his fields of interest. Yet, in at least one area, the significance of Locke's accomplishments has been drastically understated, if not completely overlooked.

In this essay, Alain Locke will be dealt with as a philosophical anthropologist. Even though Locke never identified himself as such, it is a role in which it is unlikely that he would be uncomfortable, for he espoused many of the tenets of that field of study. To be sure, one is categorizing Locke on the basis of his intellectual orientation rather than on the specifics of his academic degrees. He would have found it difficult to acquire anthropological training at

1. Robert E. Fennell, "From the Coin's Other Side: An Informal View of Alain Locke," *Recapit*, I (February, 1959), 1.

the time that he was earning his degrees, even had that been his intention, since the color line in the discipline had not yet been broken. It was only "during the 1920's [that] conditions became propitious for the first Black anthropologists to emerge."[2] Locke earned his classification as one of the select few persons who can be identified as philosophical anthropologists because he spent much of his life explicating and clarifying aspects of cultural relationships, and he repeatedly posited the necessity of developing positive inter-action between differing groups of peoples, based on a recognition of commonly shared values and concerns. Further, he was able to bring together, as few others could, ideas and action, as well as cul-ture and concepts, into a fused entity. The scope of Locke's under-standing transcended the gap between the ideal and the real.

In addition, three specific kinds of situations which further show that Locke can accurately be considered a philosophical anthropolo-gist are his actual presentation of anthropology as classroom subject matter, his stated acceptance of the value and utility of anthropo-logical thought, and his numerous writings on subjects of race, cul-ture, and group interrelationships.

Philosophical anthropology is considered to be the "German school" of anthropological thought, and it seems likely that Locke received his initial exposure to this field while studying at Berlin University in 1910, under the tutelage of Von Meinong, Brentano, and others. He may have further refined his ideas during his gradu-ate study at Harvard, where he explored the ideas of Von Ehrenfels and Hugo Munsterberg along with those of Kant and Hegel.

The substantive origins of philosophical anthropology date back to Greek philosophy, but it was during the 1920s that it was re-established as "a new, ultimate foundation, a 'transcendental phi-losophy.'"[3] The fundamental approach to the field requires study-ing man as a being determined by history, culture, and tradition and

2. St. Clair Drake, "Anthropology and the Black Experience," *Black Scholar*, II (September–October, 1980), 14.
3. Michael Landmann, *Philosophical Anthropology* (Philadelphia: Westminster Press, 1969), 9.

taking a view of the whole rather than using a fragmented analytical approach.

Philosophical anthropology is a discipline with which not a great number of people are terribly familiar. Some explanatory comments followed by a focus on some of the ideas expressed by Locke should help to illustrate why he has earned a niche as a significant figure in this field of study.

Being a transcendental area of study that employs a holistic analytical approach, philosophical anthropology attempts to establish concretely and comprehensively the constitutive basis of philosophical reality. In this field of study, man is defined in terms of his powers of abstraction, his ability to distinguish between good and evil, his place in his natural setting and his cultural world, and as mentioned previously, his susceptibility to history, culture, and tradition. The two tasks of the philosophical anthropologist are to:

1. Inquire into the fundamental ontological structures that constitute man in contrast to all other beings which exist.
2. Inquire into the nature of man in a way that those properties might be discovered which can move man to his apex.

In order to facilitate these inquiries, a basic set of assumptions can be made:

1. Man's knowledge of man is not without effect on man's being.
2. Culture is created by man's own initiative.
3. Man is the being that still has work to do on himself.
4. Self-interpretations become ideals and objectives that regulate self-formation.
5. Often man is impelled from the outside rather than self-determined.

What has been presented here about the position of philosophical anthropology in regard to the human species also applies to the individual person. In that sense, every individual and every group can increase its perfectibility by enlarging its own self-understanding. By pursuing this approach, man "retains his openness and adaptability, but he also strives constantly for completion and determinacy." [4]

4. *Ibid.*, 23.

Locke's understanding of humankind, of the various dimensions of cultural expression, and his belief in the inherent possibilities and potential of reasoned activity were constantly evidenced. He took it upon himself, as a matter of individual principle, to devote his time, energy, and intellect to exposing the absurdity of theories that elevated any group to a level of inherent superiority over another and to promoting and sustaining cultural excellence in a variety of forms. Locke's continual search for the properties that might move humanity to a higher level of development was exercised in a universalistic perspective, but with particular attention to the uplifting of black people in America.

The Harlem Renaissance could properly be regarded as the realization of Locke's belief in the maxim that man's own initiative creates the culture of which he then becomes a major part. To a significant degree, it was Locke's vision, foresight, and tireless effort that caused a germ of creativity to be extended into this epidemic of cultural outpouring. An understanding of the present, knowledge of the past, and a sense of the future made Locke at once a pragmatist and a visionary. Few persons have been as successful in bringing forth and catalyzing such significant tangible productions out of spiritual possibilities.

Self-understanding and perfectibility were the bywords of Locke's existence and of his approach to human cultural development. Locke's investigation into the positive and beneficial aspects of cultural expression moved him past the position of the observant and concerned, but uninvolved, philosopher. Likewise, his concern with man's philosophical nature and value theory in particular differentiated him from the usual culture-focused anthropologist. Because he was involved with both philosophy and culture, with ideals and interaction, and because he attempted to wed the two differentiated foci into a single, harmonious entity, Locke was, without question, a philosophical anthropologist.

When Locke accepted a teaching post at Howard University in 1912, though his classroom activities and class offerings were wide ranging, it seems likely that his interest in the study and exploration of culture would have made itself evident in his lectures and seminars, irrespective of the specific disciplinary orientation of a given course. In fact, Locke is known to have "devoted much of his own teaching to the new science of anthropology, social conflict and social theory." While his initial appointment was as professor of education and English, Locke later became professor and chairman of the Department of Philosophy at Howard. During the approximately forty years that he served as professor of philosophy, several thousand students came into contact with Locke and received the benefit of his philosophical anthropological outlook. He is, in addition, credited with introducing anthropological thinking, along with philosophy and aesthetics, into the Howard curriculum. This action coincided with the efforts of a group of anthropologists to direct the discipline toward a challenge to the rampant racism that was inherent in the social sciences. These efforts were initially led by Franz Boas and later continued by Ruth Benedict and Ashley Montagu.[5]

In *When Peoples Meet*, Locke praised anthropology for having "made available a considerable amount of fresh and illuminating material, in the light of which many doctrines that have the superficial appearance of scholarship turn out to be sophisticated versions of the fallacies and assumptions more obviously involved in popular and propagandist thinking."[6] He visualized anthropology serving as the guide and adjutant for lifting social and cultural loyalties to a plane of enlarged mutual understanding. It was Locke's feeling that through the use of anthropology, "doors would be open to such new understandings and perspectives as are necessary for the new relationships of a world order and its different juxtapositions of many different cultures."[7] A universalism based, not on com-

5. Eugene C. Holmes, "The Legacy of Alain Locke," *Freedomways*, (Summer, 1963), n.p.; Eugene C. Holmes, from a presentation read at a memorial meeting for Alain Locke held at New York University on October 29, 1955, rpr. *Journal of Philosophy*, LIV (February 28, 1957), 113; Drake, "Anthropology and the Black Experience," 3–4.

6. Alain Locke and Bernard Stern (eds.), *When Peoples Meet* (New York: Progressive Education Association, 1942), 4–5.

7. Alain Locke, "Cultural Relativism and Ideological Peace," in *Approaches to World Peace* (New York: Fourth Symposium of the Conference on Science, Philosophy, and Religion, 1944), 612.

monality of opinions and points of view, but on mutual respect and appreciation of differences, was the goal Locke projected for the world. He held the belief that peoples of different persuasions could meet, settle their differences amicably, then turn their attention to building a better existence. Locke deplored the domination of the world arena by movements or programs whose interests and concerns were for their betterment and expansion, even to the point of ignoring or overlooking the viewpoints and considerations of other groups, movements, or individuals.

Throughout his writings, Locke repeatedly echoes ideas and concerns that are at the very heart of philosophical anthropological thought. He "amply demonstrates that the professional philosopher has something significant to say on questions of cultural presuppositions." Locke fuses his philosophical orientation and his consideration of various issues of race and culture with extraordinary objectivity, analysis, and insight. "In common with other contemporary philosophers, such as Alfred North Whitehead, Ernst Cassirer, and John Dewey, he maintains that the major cultures of the Western and the Eastern worlds involve basic theoretical assumptions from which the social institutions and practices that they value proceed." [8]

Thus, a definitive link is established, in Locke's judgment, between the principles and precepts on which man bases his actions and the structural mechanisms that are developed to carry out those actions. The clear relationship between the theoretical constructs that both mandate and restrict behavior patterns and the facilitative appendages that guide and channel social activities, means that modification and change can be effected at the philosophical level and then actualized through various social institutions. Given such a clearly identified integrative operation, leaders of different constituent groups, utilizing objective judgment, could be the architects of a new social order designed on principles of social symbiosis. In addition, barriers of religious, political, economic, and

8. David Bidney, *Theoretical Anthropology* (New York: Schocken Books, 1970), 169, 170.

ethnic difference, while not removed, would be lessened in significance by the identification of and subscription to a more fundamental set of common concerns and interests. Locke's projections
are perhaps closer to actualization than one might immediately
think, considering the development, within the past few years,
of such policies and slogans as *detente, rapprochement,* and *global
interdependence.*

As a means of reducing bias and subjectivity in the comparison
of cultures, Locke called for a method of relative scientific grading
of cultures in his essay, "The Concept of Race as Applied to Social
Culture." Lest his position be confused with that taken by Lewis
Morgan, Herbert Spencer, Edward Tylor, and the evolutionist
school of anthropology, he presents two clarifying concepts for the
study of any culture. "First, its analytic and complete description in
terms of its own culture-elements, second, its organic interpretation in terms of its own intrinsic values as a vital mode of living,
combined if possible with an historical account of its development
and derivation."[9] This statement is an early allusion to Locke's notion of cultural relativity, an idea which, along with his call for an
objective evaluation of cultures, occurs repeatedly in his writings.
He felt that a thorough knowledge of another culture was necessary
to understand its intricacies, which to the outsider may appear to be
oddities. Factors such as racial prejudice would then be minimized
in examining other cultures when a culturally relativistic approach
was used.

The concept of cultural relativity is, in fact, used by Locke to
bridge the gap between the abstractness of value-theory and the
preciseness of culture theory, and as a negation of absolutism in either of these two areas. He writes in "Values and Imperatives" that
"the effective antidote to value absolutism lies in a systematic and
realistic demonstration that values are rooted in attitudes, not in reality, and pertain to ourselves, not to the world." Thus, his call for
value pluralism as a sensible philosophical position is totally con-

9. Alain Locke, "The Concept of Race as Applied to Social Culture," *Howard
Review,* I (June, 1924), 299.

sistent with his support of cultural pluralism as a worthwhile anthropological approach. Locke's philosophical and anthropological
postures blend into a unitary flow of thought, directed towards in-
creased understanding and against absolutism of any kind. Acknowledging the fusion of the two areas of thought is Locke's comment that "cultural relativism, to my mind, is the culminating
phase of relativistic philosophy, and it is bound to have a greater
influence than any other phase of relativism upon our conception
and practice of values."[10] As a firm believer in the ultimate sanctity
of the shared modes of the human experience, Locke assailed dogmatic ideologies that presented one group of people or set of values
as being superior to others. The relativistic approach advocated by
Locke, for all intents and purposes, renders meaningless exagger-
ated claims of superiority, especially in regard to values and belief
systems.

For Locke, though, relativism was not the end in itself but a
means of reaching a universality that rests on the twin bases of objectivity and tolerance. In "Pluralism and Intellectual Democracy,"
he contended that if relativism "could discover beneath the expected culture differentials of time and place such functional 'universals' as actually may be there, these common–denominator values would stand out as pragmatically confirmed by common
human experience."[11] At the core of the human experience and
basic to group interaction, Locke felt, is a body of shared elemental
notions that transcend geography and particular patterns of social
development. He contended that absolutism had obscured these
common values and that relativism presented an opportunity to
bring them forth as a basis for broadening understanding between
various peoples.

The relativist point of view, then, is a pragmatic approach to
bridging the differences between culture groups and value orienta-

10. Alain Locke, "Values and Imperatives," in Horace Meyer Kallen and Sidney
Hook (eds.), *American Philosophy, Today and Tomorrow* (New York: Lee Furman,
1935), 328, 331.
11. Alain Locke, "Pluralism and Intellectual Democracy," in *Second Symposium*
(New York: Conference on Science, Philosophy, and Religion, 1942), 200.

tions according to Locke, because it "equips us not only to tolerate differences but enables us to bridge divergence by recognizing commonality wherever present . . . it puts the premium on equivalence not upon identity, calls for co-operation rather than for conformity and promotes reciprocity instead of factional antagonism."[12] The logic of Locke's argument is inescapable. But, though his relativistic approach is functional both in intent and result, it can only be regarded in this conflict-ridden world as being idealistic in its orientation. In a sense, the irony of Locke's approach to a resolution of human problems is that it demands that all parties not only reiterate their own humanity but acknowledge the humanity of others as well. While we have seen some limited steps taken in this direction, it may be that Locke's articulation of relativism is much more reflective of the man himself and his conception of a satisfying life than of the multitudes who lack his vision and wisdom.

As a philosophical anthropologist, Locke accepted the premise that man's idea of himself becomes the ideal that shapes and guides him, though his interpretation of himself does not stand separate from an immutable reality.[13] This is why the approach that he advocated for the attainment of universal understanding had at its foundation the recognition of the parity of cultures. He explained how this realization could occur: "We cannot in any reasonably near future envisage any substantial lessening of the differences in our basic value systems, either philosophical or cultural. The only viable alternative seems, therefore, not to expect to change others but to change our attitudes toward them, and to seek rapprochment [sic] not by the eradication of such differences as there are but by schooling ourselves not to make so much of the differences."[14]

Locke could have hardly been more specific in mapping out the path to a better world. Writing as an intellectual analyst to one of the most educated nations in the world, it would seem that the clar-

12. *Ibid.*, 205.
13. Landmann, *Philosophical Anthropology*, 23.
14. Alain Locke, "Pluralism and Ideological Peace," in Sidney Hook and Milton R. Konvitz (eds.), *Freedom and Experience* (Ithaca: Cornell University Press, 1947), 64.

ity of his pronouncements might have evoked some serious consideration from social planners and concerned leaders. But despite the
brilliance of his insights and observations, Locke's words went un-
heeded, and this blueprint for global harmony received little serious
consideration. It may be that in this, and other instances as well,
Locke's blackness precluded his receiving the attention from race-
conscious white America that he so obviously deserved, or it may
be that Locke was, quite simply, a man who was ahead of his time.
In the same essay, Locke clarifies his concept of universalism as
being that of a "fluid and functional unity that begins in a basic
progression of value pluralism, converts itself to value relativism as
its only consistent interpretation, and then passes over into a ready
and willing admission of both cultural relativism and pluralism." [15]
The fundamental equivalence of cultures, irrespective of their particular process of development, is a significant underlying aspect of
Locke's universalism and a key component of its distinct pluralistic focus.

What one finds in Locke then, is a continuous effort to direct the
collective energies of all peoples toward a transcendental approach
to interaction in which differences of race, culture, values, and ideas
are respected and appreciated. In focusing on the threads of common experiences and concerns, he believed that human beings can
construct a world order that draws its strength from the implicit
similarities of the human experience. Here again, Locke can be seen
as a philosophical anthropologist, for his view of culture is "from
an intellectual perspective as essentially an ideology, or system of
ideas." [16] His analysis leads him to conclude that from a functional
standpoint, those ideas can and should coexist on a basis of parity
and relativity.

Along with the idea of cultural equivalence, Locke detailed two
other principles that he felt were important "for a more objective
and scientific understanding of human cultures and for the more
reasonable control of their inter-relationships."

15. *Ibid.*, 65.
16. Bidney, *Theoretical Anthropology*, 412.

1. The principle of cultural reciprocity, which acknowledges the highly composite nature of all modern cultures.

2. The principle of limited cultural convertibility, which acknowledges that the organic selectivity and assimilative capacity of a borrowing culture becomes a limiting criterion for cultural exchange.[17]

Cultural reciprocity implies a kind of building-block approach to the developmental process. It suggests that cultures germinate around concerns that are fundamental to that particular group of persons, then extend outward to envelop other concerns or ideas that are peripheral to that culture. A central focus for one culture may be an insignificant one for another culture, but both cultures manage to meet the primary and peripheral needs of its citizens. In that sense, the cultures are reciprocal, even though they may be highly differentiated in design and focus. Reciprocity between cultures suggests a basic equality, predicated on substantive results rather than surface appearance.

On the other hand, the idea of limited cultural convertibility functions on the premise that a given culture, though it may openly or discreetly borrow certain concepts or mechanisms from another culture, is limited in the amount that it can take from elsewhere for internal use. Factors, which vary from one place to another, exist which limit the utility of more than a certain quantity of material, whether physical or conceptual, that can be absorbed into a given cultural system. As a result, the idea of cultural exchange can be operationalized only to a certain level. The effect is that no culture can ever be completely absorbed or erased by another, even though it might be dominated for extended periods of time.

The three principles of cultural relations were important elements in Locke's overall platform for global harmony. He believed that these principles, if generally acknowledged, "might correct some of our basic culture dogmatism and progressively cure many of our most intolerant and prejudicial culture attitudes and practices."[18]

17. Locke, "Cultural Relativism," 613.
18. Ibid., 614.

If humans are to be moved to their apex through the discovery and use of certain properties, and this is a motive that is significant among philosophical anthropologists, certainly self-knowledge is one of those properties with which they would be most concerned. But it is not enough to know self; we must know others as well. And for Locke, the only sensible way to know and understand others is "by first disestablishing the use of one's own culture as a contrast norm for other cultures, which leads through the appreciation of the functional significance of other values in their respective cultures to the eventual discovery and recognition of certain functional common denominators."[19]

It was Locke's relentless search for those common denominators—those modes of behavior and expression that cannot be masked even by the circumstances of adaptation—that completes his identification and underscores his significance as a philosophical anthropologist. His persistent efforts to construct a unitary framework within which differences in values, race, and culture would exist in harmonious relationship establishes his contribution to this field of study. Locke conceptualized the goal of a mosaic tapestry of different peoples and cultures, woven with the threads of understanding and mutual respect. He contributed both a vision and an ideal which, if we have the wisdom and courage to pursue them, might lead to the kind of world in which weapons are replaced by reason. Among his many other contributions to humanity, this very important one is too often overlooked.

And despite its low level of recognition, even in the academic community, "philosophical anthropology has survived both as a school of philosophy and as a methodological viewpoint outside of philosophy."[20] Locke appears to have been both comfortable and proficient in both of the operational modes. The legacy that Alain Locke has bequeathed to the generations that follow him is one of rational thought, dispassionate critical analysis, and undying hope in the ultimate emergence of reason over prejudice.

19. *Ibid.*, 617.
20. Landmann, *Philosophical Anthropology*, 11.

Relativism and Pluralism in the Social Thought of Alain Locke

RUTLEDGE M. DENNIS

Since the United States is, more than most countries, a nation of immigrants, much theoretical as well as practical attention has been focused on assumptions regarding the forms of "ideal" relations between racial and cultural groups and how such group relations could constitute the basis for a coherent national sociocultural unit. In general, the question of group stratification was posed along bipolar dimensions—groups would either melt in the assimilation process or sustain themselves in a state of pluralistic interdependency. Anglo-Saxon chauvinism viewed the assimilationist theory as one in which other groups would give up their cultural tradition to follow Anglo-Saxon values. Thus Anglo-Saxon conformity would represent a form of Anglo-Saxon value superiority and dominance. This view can be juxtaposed with the pluralist vision of the various strains of Afro-American nationalism and the nationalism of the various white ethnic groups.

Before the turn of the twentieth century, W. E. B. Du Bois had called for the acceptance of cultural diversity in his article, "On the Conservation of Races." His classic model of the "double conscious" was, in this article, stated in the ambivalent terms of "Am I an American or am I a Negro? . . . Can I be both?" The tenor of both his life and his writings supports the view that Du Bois answered yes to the question "Can I be both?" Du Bois, however, was not the first black thinker to pose the question, nor was he the last, since the question has implicitly been a part of the psychosocial experience of blacks since their arrival in North and South America. Marcus Garvey was later to speak to the issue of racial and cultural diversity as an acknowledgment of the great African past and promising Pan-African future.[1] Both his and Du Bois' concern with pluralism and diversity centered on practical and programmatic activities that would enable blacks to challenge and confront white Americans in the Du Boisian sense and to build an independent existence for global Pan-Africanism in Garveyan terms. Thus, though both Du Bois and Garvey were committed to different cultural and political paradigms, they were similarly committed to a program of social action.

Alain Locke, unlike Du Bois and Garvey, approached cultural pluralism and diversity with a special view toward the delineation and clarification of the concepts and issues germane to the particularisms of black sociocultural survival. When Locke began to publish his critical analysis of pluralism and relativism, these terms had already become a part of the intellectual jargon of the day. Their origins can be traced to the philosophical and scientific framework posited by the philosopher and psychologist William James. James and Charles Pierce posed the philosophical question of ideas as relative to time and place, thus divesting philosophy of any claim of absolutism.[2] Their idea of the flux and flow of reality was the central theme in the distinctly American philosophy of pragmatism. James's attack on philosophical and methodological monism, and his definition of truth as that which is useful, helped to lead the attack against monism and absolutism in the social and cultural spheres. Just as James reasoned that philosophical and methodological pluralism would produce a wider and more comprehen-

1. Julius Lester (ed.), *The Seventh Son: The Thought and Writings of W. E. B. Du Bois* (2 vols.; New York: Random House, 1971), I, 182; Marcus Garvey, *The Philosophy and Opinions of Marcus Garvey* (London: Frank Cass, 1967), 21.
2. John K. Roth (ed.), *The Moral Philosophy of William James* (New York: Thomas Crowell, 1969), 295.

sive search for scientific unity, he believed that the idea of a plural society would be crucial in the formation of philosophical and social humanism.

John Dewey followed in the philosophical pluralist footsteps of James, but he was to develop a more definite link between pluralism and immigrant groups, and between pluralism and democracy. Thus, "many truths" became many groups and many realities became the basis for viewing many cultures. Linking pluralism and democracy, Dewey stated: "A democracy is more than a form of government, it is primarily a mode of associated living, of conjoint communicated experience." Dewey's declarations against cultural conformity and social homogeneity were partially based on his rural New England upbringing and what he perceived to be the widespread urban social disorganization and anomie prevalent in cities such as Chicago and New York. In protesting against the industrialized urban society and against what is often called "mass society," Dewey posited the idea of "a plural society made up of any number of self regulating communities, all open to the larger world and taking part in a dialogue of shared intelligence with other communities."[3]

Locke utilizes the intellectual scaffold of James and Dewey, but he was to gain a firsthand account of pluralism from Horace Kallen, who coined the term *cultural pluralism*. Kallen had first used the term in 1906 or 1907, when he worked as an assistant in a class taught by George Santayana.[4] Like Kallen, Locke focused his analysis of pluralism on the idea of democracy and culture, and like Kallen, his views must be viewed with respect to the national and international racial and cultural conflicts of the 1920s, 30s, and 40s. Just as Kallen was particularly interested in pluralism as it related to the variegated forms of Jewish particularisms, Locke's interest was focused on Afro-American particularisms. Each sought to de-

3. Seymour W. Itzkoff, *Cultural Pluralism and American Education* (Scranton: International Textbook, 1970), 42, 46.
4. Horace Kallen, "Alain Locke and Cultural Pluralism," *Journal of Philosophy*, LIV (1957), 119.

mythologize and demystify the idea of democracy as only implying
a majority role in which minorities would be voiceless.

Locke's Conceptual and Philosophical Framework

Like James, Dewey, and Kallen, Locke juxtaposed the pluralist conceptual ideal against that of the assimilationist-monist conceptual
ideal. An analysis of Locke's writings reveals certain conceptual and
schematic patterns, which may be grouped in categories for clearer
codification. Representing Locke's idea of the polar extremes in political government, the following diagram dichotomizes and de-
picts the relationship between democracy and totalitarianism. The
diagram might be said to represent a Weberian ideal typology in
that the use of terms seen as pure types are never really in the same
form as they would be in the real world, though Locke did view,
and sought to explain, these concepts with reference to the conflicts
between the democracies and fascism and nazism of the 1920s, 30s,
and 40s.[5]

Democracy	Totalitarianism
Leads to:	Leads to:
Pluralism	Monism
Cultural relativism	Anarchic relativism
Objectivity	Subjectivity
Rationalism	Emotionalism
Cultural reciprocity	Cultural chauvinism
Political divergence	Political absolutism

The one concept that Locke used with great care was that of particularity. In general this idea can be used in contrast to universality
and cosmopolitanism, but Locke always attempted to state that particularisms had to be kept carefully within reasonable bounds lest
they spill over into forms of chauvinism. It is perhaps for this reason that Locke seemed more intent on moving from the particular,

5. Alain Locke, "Pluralism and Ideological Peace," in Sidney Hook and Milton
R. Konvitz (eds.), *Freedom and Experience* (Ithaca: Cornell University Press, 1947),
63.

even in a modest sense, to a form of universality.[6] Though he considered the particulars important (particular groups, values, etc.), he appears to have expressed the ideas of logic and reason in universalist terms. This particular point can probably be viewed as an example of Locke's ambivalence. On the other hand, it might also be viewed as simply the oscillatory nature of the concept when its applications are tested in the real world. It is one thing to dichotomize the world in the abstract, and it is yet another to test the degree to which formal constructs conform to some features of what actually happens "out there"; and like Dewey and Kallen, Locke's philosophical framework had a great bearing on some sociological issues he wanted to address. But Locke seemed never to want to remain completely in the realm of either the universal or the particular.

Locke assumed that democracy would lead to freedom and the liberation of individuals and groups and that totalitarianism would lead to the denial of individual and group rights. Having said this, it is important to repeat that Locke did not believe that the then existing democracies were practicing the ideals of pluralism, objectivity, and rationality, though the then existing totalitarian governments were, in fact, displaying emotionality, subjectivity, and absolutism in their campaign against other racial groups.[7] But one cannot mention this fact without noting the undemocratic and totalitarian methods by which native Americans and Afro-Americans had been subjugated and continued to be subjugated while intellectuals sought an explication of pluralism. We can thus speak of the "relative" degree to which either democracy or totalitarianism may adhere to the labels placed upon them; some of the concepts used to describe each type of government might be more appropriate than others. Although it does appear that items listed under democracy in the table above are more ideals and goals of the system rather than existing realities, both democracy and totalitarianism would certainly fit the category of "ideal types."

6. Alain Locke, "The New Negro," in Locke (ed.), *The New Negro* (New York: Albert and Charles Boni, 1925), 14.
7. Alain Locke, "Unity Through Diversity: A Baha'i Principle," *Baha'i World*, IV (1930), 373.

Culture and Group Values

Locke's interest in cultural coexistence certainly considered the existing political, economic, and cultural inequalities between racial, religious, and language groups, but one sees in his writings on culture that he was interested in validating the black cultural reality sui generis and not merely as a manifestation of reaction to white oppression. That is, the analysis of group values and cultural motifs may suggest less dependency than both dominant and less dominant groups might presuppose. In fact, the idea of cultural maintenance and value stability as transformative entities was clearly enunciated by Locke. For example, he viewed the quest for cultural autonomy as intricately linked to the psychosocial development of blacks, and though this development can be seen apart from problem solving per se, it stands parallel to the claims that blacks have on the larger society. He spoke to this point in his essay, "The New Negro":

> The Old Negro . . . has been a stock figure perpetuated as an historical fiction partly in innocent sentimentalism, partly in deliberate reactionism. The Negro himself has contributed his share to this through a sort of protective social mimicry forced upon him by the adverse circumstances of dependence . . . the thinking Negro even has been induced to share this same general attitude to focus his attention on controversial issues, to see himself in the distorted perspective of a social problem. His shadow, so to speak, has been more real to him than his personality. Through having to appeal from the unjust stereotypes of his oppressors and traducers to those of his liberators, friends and benefactors, he has had to subscribe to the traditional positions from which his case has been viewed. Little true social or self-understanding has or could come from such a situation.[8]
> . . . .
> The Negro today is inevitably moving forward under the control largely of his own objectives. What are these objectives? Those of his outer life are happily already well and finally formulated, for they are none other than the ideals of American institutions and democracy. Those of his inner life are yet in process of for-

8. Locke, "The New Negro," 3–4.

mation, for the new psychology at present is more of a consensus of feeling than of opinion, of attitude than of program. . . . This deep feeling of race is at present the mainspring of Negro life . . . it is radical in tone, but not in purpose.[9]

Thus the central problem of cultural fulfillment cannot be seen *in toto*, devoid of the constraining force that helps to shape group reality, but as Ralph Ellison asserts, no group is *merely* the result of its reaction to external constraints by others. Ellison speaks to the fact that even with the severe historical oppression, blacks indeed have been capable of making "a life upon the horns of the white man's dilemma.[10] What Locke's quotations refer to are the subterfuges and deceptions that have been traditional aspects of black life when confronted by white economic and political power. The "New Negro" is in the process of emerging, and this emergence has its roots in the psychological and sociological mainstreams of black life. Locke also appears to be saying that life and culture are one; that culture emerges from a people's inner world and works to reinforce every aspect of that world. This is why he was interested in explicating the New Negro in the United States and analyzing the emergence of totalitarian cultures in Europe. These analyses might help to answer key questions he posed:

1. What is the process by which sociocultural values are acquired?
2. What is the process by which sociocultural values are transmitted?
3. Once transmitted, how can cultural ties be strengthened?
4. Why do individuals and societies accept value positions that are racially chauvinistic?
5. How can societies create and promote universalistic rather than particularistic value systems?

Answers to these questions would require extensive systematic empirical research. In other words, the usefulness of philosophical deduction, whereas quite fruitful in explication, analysis, and systematization, is limited when more specific questions are raised. Locke, despite his positing of these questions in the sociological

9. *Ibid.*, 10–11.
10. Ralph Ellison, *Shadow and Act* (New York: Random House, 1964), 315.

vein, really had no vehicle with which to answer them inasmuch as he, like James and the other pragmatists, was highly critical of the then growing movement towards positivism and radical empiricism. The answers are not, however, farfetched according to the research standards of traditional anthropology, nor are they inconsistent with a Lewinian brand of social research on group culture and the idea of value reconstruction.[11] In the case of the latter, the concern is a massive restructuring of social values. Obviously, this is no easy task. In the Germany described by Lewin, only war, destruction, and the imposition of law by the Allied powers altered Nazi ideology; and though Locke was not to live long enough to see it, it took national judicial decisions and various congressional acts to alter some basic structural inequalities in the American social and educational system. A case can be made that Americans have not fully attacked all of the problems in these areas.

Locke approached the problems of values and culture with insights culled from two separate spheres: his view of himself as a "cultural cosmopolitan" on one hand, and on the other as an advocate of "cultural racialism." One can make a case that there is an inherent contradiction in being both cosmopolitan and racialist, as did Kallen.[12] But, to refer back to a previous point, the two terms may well be viewed as ideal types, and hence abstract; but in the real world of values and cultures what might contradict on the formal, logical plane may blend in unusual configurations in everyday life. This, of course, speaks to the unusual degree to which people live on the theoretical (belief patterns) level but are able to suppress certain elements of this level when they confront the demands of everyday life. Locke was to write to himself in paradoxical and contradictory terms:

> Philadelphia . . . at the start set the key of paradox; circumstance compounded it by decreeing me as a Negro, a dubious and doubting sort of American and by reason of the racial inheritance

11. Kurt Lewin, *Resolving Social Conflicts* (New York: Harper and Brothers, 1948), 37.
12. Kallen, "Alain Locke and Cultural Pluralism," 123.

making me more of a pagan than a puritan, more of a humanist than a pragmatist . . . socially Anglophile, but because of race loyalty, strenuously anti-imperialist, universalist in religion, internationalist and pacifist in world-view, but forced by a sense of simple justice to approve of the militant counter-nationalisms of Zionism, Young Turkey, Young Egypt, Young India, and with reservation even Garveyism and current day "Nippon over Asia." Finally a cultural racialism as a defensive counter-movement for the American Negro.[13]

Though he does not pose questions of identity, as did Du Bois, Locke viewed his paradoxes as social and, by inference, personal. But he understood the human dilemma and the difficulty of value reconstruction, for restructuring had to pass the emotional sensors of people whose sentiments might not be in accordance with change. Pinpointing the problem, he noted that "we feel and hope in the direction of universality, but still think and act particularistically."

The Social and the Psychological

Locke was interested in the psychological (cognitive) dispositions that he thought important in predetermining attitude or behavior toward a group or a value. He viewed these as contrasts between the rational approach and the emotional approach. He described human behavior as "selectively preferential" and guided by emotional preferences and affinities. In what appears to be a pessimistic resignation of the rational to the emotional, Locke stated in Nietzschean terms: "Our varied absolutes are revealed as largely the rationalization of our preferred values and their imperatives. Their tap-root, it seems, stems more from the will to power than from the will to know. Little can be done, it would appear, either toward their explanation or their reconciliation on the rational plane."[14] Though the reference to the will takes on biological as well as psychological meanings, Locke did not overlook sociologi-

13. Alain Locke, "Values and Imperatives," in Horace Meyer Kallen and Sidney Hook (eds.), *American Philosophy, Today and Tomorrow* (New York: Lee Furman, 1935), 312.
14. *Ibid.*, 328.

cal factors. In fact he said that ideological factors are embedded in the institutions of the society. That is, they are sociological in nature. In general, Locke tended not to rely on factors such as the "will to power." He tended to blend psychological and sociological explanations. For example, in a broadside attack on the common man, Locke talked about the "blind practicality of the common man . . . who . . . in both his individual and group behavior, perpetuates the problem of universal fundamentalism. . . . He sets up personal and private and group norms as standards and principles, and rightly or wrongly hypostasizes them as universals for all conditions, all times and all men." But we have been prepared for Locke's denouncement of the common man by his statement in "The New Negro" that "the only safeguard for mass relations and race relations in the future must be provided in the carefully maintained contacts of the enlightened minorities of both race groups." [15]

Sociologically and psychologically Locke was saying that once racial ideology becomes embedded in social institutions and in the minds of the people, it is difficult to uproot that ideology. At that point, cultural and political socialization occurs as a result of the family, peer groups, schools, social groups, and mass media. Locke stated that individuals derive personal ego satisfaction from *feelings* of cultural and value superiority over other individuals in other groups. But Locke continued without adequate clarification to write of the ubiquity of certain types of group inequalities: "There are and always will be specialized group superiorities." [16] Such a position appears to undercut his assumptions of the need not to enunciate ideas of group superiority or inferiority, especially as they might cloud the issue and promote even more inequalities. He pursued this point in a 1944 essay and, again without carefully explaining how scientific objectivity can be used to measure inferiority or superiority, writes as if the reality of such were a foregone conclusion: "Claims of cultural superiority or counter-judgments of cul-

15. *Ibid.*, 315; Locke, "The New Negro," 9.
16. Alain Locke, "The Contribution of Race to Culture," *Student World* (1950), 351.

tural inferiority would be specific and carefully circumscribed and would be significant and allowable if substantiated by fair, objective comparison. For I take it, we would not disallow such judgmental valuations as might stem from an objectively scientific criterion of more or less effective adaptation."[17]

We can assume, of course, that Locke's previous logic had backed him into this corner, because one of the bases for his denouncement of racial chauvinism and group comparison is that the comparison is inherently *arbitrary* and *subjective*. The supposition seems to be then that if objective techniques are constructed, we will be able to objectively assess different cultures. The danger here is that we are not given the "how." Nowhere did Locke explicitly state what the criterion should be or how assessments and comparisons can ever be made. Locke led us to the foot of the mountain, but refused to give us the rope to make it to the top. One of the weaknesses in Locke's sociological orientation to pluralism and relativism was his failure to analyze group relations vis-à-vis power and power relations. It is not that one expects him to be a sociologist or a political scientist, but given his immense output in the area of group relations, one expects a deeper fleshing out of the issues. In such instances it becomes ever so evident that Locke was a philosopher, and we should not allow his sociological insights to lull us into expecting deep sociological probings. It is here that Locke's idealism emerged for the posited group values as opposed to the group itself. He posited values rather than power as the independent variable; therefore, from his analysis it appears as if *values* alone can cause groups to be dominated, rather than the combination of political and economic power in addition to cultural ideological factors. It is not, however, mere values that cause domination; it is when values are directed towards tangible objects and groups that social differentiation and social equality take place. So without indicting Locke for being what he made no disclaimers to be—a phi-

17. Alain Locke, "Cultural Relativism and Ideological Peace," in *Approaches to World Peace* (New York: Fourth Symposium of the Conference on Science, Philosophy, and Religion, 1944), 614.

losopher—one nevertheless wishes that he had conducted as careful a scrutiny of power (or the lack of) as a precipitator of cultural inequality and other socioeconomic inequalities as he had done with his general philosophical analysis of values.

Cosmopolitanism and Parochialism

It would appear that any discussion of cosmopolitanism and parochialism would automatically juxtapose these terms as dichotomous and therefore contradictory. Locke's analysis of the term did not, however, suggest any such extreme bipolarity. It was precisely his position that the universal and the particular may unite to ground individuals and groups more firmly in a specific culture while at the same time offer a wider parameter by which new insights into, or a wider dimension of, social life might be achieved. To give up one's own way of life in pursuit of cosmopolitanism is to forsake the sense of the historical, cultural, and racial self. But to burrow one's self too deeply in the parochialism of one's own cultural motifs is to lose sight of the richness of the cultural mosiac that enlightens and allows for cultural and social transcendentalism. He thus accepted the universal and the particular, but with equal qualifications: "Personally I belong to such a minority, and have had some part in the revival of its suppressed hopes; but if I thought it irreconcilable with the future development of internationalism and the approach toward universalism to foster the racial sense, stimulate the racial consciousness and help revive the lapsing racial tradition, I would count myself a dangerous reactionary, and be ashamed of what I still think is a worthy and constructive cause."[18]

Locke seemed to have been working to achieve a balance between the Scylla of potential alienation from a too hasty movement toward cosmopolitanism and the Charybdis of deadening cultural narrowness through the constraints of parochialism. Thus, according to this logic it is possible to argue a case for a dynamic cultural nationalism that feeds and touches upon, but is not extinguished by, cosmopolitanism. The idea of cosmopolitan nationalism is seman-

18. Locke, "The Contribution of Race to Culture," 350.

tically contradictory, but the process is dialectical. Locke's dilemma was that he was uneasy with the potential negativisms of racialism, and yet he was unwilling to give it up. "If we argue for raciality as a desirable thing, we seem to argue for the present practice of nations and to sanction the pride and prejudice of past history. Whereas, if we condemn these things, we seem close to a rejection of race as something useful in human life and desirable to perpetuate."[19] And, "We must live in terms of our own particular institution and mores, assert and cherish our own specific values, and we could not, even if it were desirable, uproot our own tradition and loyalties."[20]

The interface between the cosmopolitan and the parochial in Lockean thought, and his unwillingness to plant himself in either corner but rather to place himself in middle ground, is consistent with Locke's acceptance of the Grecian idea of nothing in excess.[21] But placing himself on middle ground did not necessarily suggest that Locke did not theoretically or practically prefer, in the end, one position above the other. Locke's writings indicate that he did, in fact, prefer the cosmopolitan to the parochial. "The cosmopolitan should share the loyalties of the group, but upon a different plane and with a higher perspective. He must partake of partisanship in order to work toward its transformation, and help keep it within the bounds of constructive and controlled self-assertion."[22] This view is congruent with Locke's perception of cosmopolitanism as analogous to an orientation to "the larger integration of life." But though he saw cosmopolitanism as enlightening, he did not believe that adherence to it would result in "complete cultural uniformity or common-mindedness about values." Ironically, Locke even argued that the cultural tolerance that results from genuine cosmopolitan ideals will increase cultural pluralism and enhance a positive parochialism.[23] According to Locke, this promotes "harmony in contrariety," which is understood if things are kept in bal-

19. *Ibid.*
20. Alain Locke, "Pluralism and Intellectual Democracy," in *Second Symposium* (New York: Conference on Science, Philosophy, and Religion, 1942), 204.
21. Locke, "Values and Imperatives," 319.
22. Locke, "Unity Through Diversity," 373.
23. Locke, "Values and Imperatives," 333.

ance. The balance would supposedly emerge as a result of understanding and respecting group differences, which would negate cultural extremism. The shifting between the universal and the particular does not seem to be an easy task, but this apparent form of "double consciousness" was not seen by Locke as individually or collectively fatal.

Philosophical Methodology

Philosophy, like many areas in the social sciences, began in the twentieth century to search for a method that was not merely speculative but, rather, systematic. During Locke's years at Harvard, the two main philosophical schools were Hegelianism and pragmatism. Thus it is possible for Locke to have accepted the substance of the pragmatists' ideas and the logical structure of the Hegelians'. Confirmation of this assumption comes from Locke himself who stated that he wanted to do his Ph.D. under the philosopher Josiah Royce but did not, and instead studied value theory under Ralph Barton Perry. Indeed, Santayana's description of Royce seems an adequate description of Locke: "He viewed everything in relation to something else . . . out of which the thing under view, if good, arises by a sort of Hegelian implication." Kallen described Royce's training in the use of the Hegelian dialectical technique and said that it signified that "life and the good of life are the struggle between good and evil, and the struggle can not be unless evil exist, the peer of good."[24] This is exactly what Locke appeared to be doing with the terms *cosmopolitanism* and *parochialism*, for he pitted one concept against the other and explained one by zeroing in on its opposite. Such an explication of concepts by definitional clarity is quite common in the social sciences. Locke does this with his multiple juxtaposition of such polarities as monism-pluralism, objectivity-subjectivity, and feeling-thinking. One even gets a hint of the Hegelian synthesis when Locke explains the movement from narrow fanatical particularism (the thesis) to relativism (the antithesis) to universalism (the synthesis).

24. Horace Kallen, *Culture and Democracy in the United States* (New York: Boni and Liveright, 1924), 300, 301.

The call for a philosophical methodology was in harmony with the general thrust of academic and professional disciplines at the turn of the century. Locke's exhortations for a scientific approach to values and cultures was not to be the version of scientific methodology that was fast becoming the preeminent method—radical empiricism. He rejected this method as arbitrary and dogmatic. He believed that the empiricist movement had fallen "increasingly into the hands of the empirical monists, who in the cause of scientific objectivity, squeezed values and ideals out completely in a fanatical cult of 'fact.'" Locke advocated a form of empiricism that would not tilt in the direction of radical positivism, but would instead work in harmony with the more traditional value disciplines such as philosophy and religion. Such a concession by science would, he believed, rid both philosophy and religion of their dogmatic absolutism. How would this be done? Locke suggested the use of an historical-comparative method. He reasoned that a comparative analysis of values and cultures would help to explain cultural and value origins. In comparing cultures and value motifs, the analyst (if unbiased) can shed light on cross-cultural similarities and dissimilarities by pointing out "functional constants." Functional constants were seen by Locke as those value similarities that transcend nationalities and races. According to this logic, all societies have certain basic values that guide their institutional growth and determine societal behavioral patterns. Consequently, if studies can reveal these constants, groups and nations may then be able to note how common forms of institutional life permeate all cultures. The result is that one form that a people might view as very unique is, in reality, similar in origin and function to a form in another society. These constants, Locke claims, are to "take scientifically the place of our outmoded categoricals and our banned arbitrary 'universals.'"[25] Here Locke put quotation marks around the word *universals*, and we can assume that the term *arbitrary universals* can only be used as an opposite of his *true universals*.

Locke's call for comparative group analysis was rather unique

25. Locke, "Pluralism and Intellectual Democracy," 197, 199.

from the cultural pluralistic perspective. Traditional pluralists such as Kallen and James had inveighed against such comparative possibilities, because they took the position that each event or experience must be acknowledged for what it appears to be, and heard for its own claim. Such a position may seem to border on a relativism that some would say approaches anarchy. If each cultural and value position is only to be assessed on its own merits and claims, then there is no way comparative analyses can be made. Locke, however, was not convinced that value relativism should be taken that far. His advocacy of the scientific approach implies that, though sympathetic to the claims of each group, he was not sure that we could not demarcate that which was good or bad, wise or unwise in each group's value orientation. Thus, his acceptance of cultural relativism and pluralism did not negate the possibility of analyzing and assessing the *content* of group culture. According to Locke, viewing a group's values only from the standpoint of its internal logic would, in fact, make it virtually impossible to make any claims against the genocidal policies of Hitler's Germany or the discriminatory policies of the United States. The need to assess content would, according to Locke, provide opposition to value monists and absolutists.[36]

Locke's advocacy of a normative philosophy using the historical-comparative approach has yet another important feature for group values: it speaks to the view of culture as a dynamic rather than a static element in society, for to oppose absolutism and cultural rigidity is to see culture as flexible and changing. It also suggests that cultural shifts are not independent of human decision making. If people create cultures, Locke's underlying assumptions contend, why shouldn't people be able to create cultural values that are, in some sense, universally functional and "good"? Thus to determine what might be functional or good is to assume that one is in a position to assess accurately cultural functions and cultural survival

26. Alain Locke, "The Need for a New Organon in Education," in *Goals for American Education* (New York: Ninth Symposium of the Conference on Science, Philosophy, and Religion, 1950), 209.

needs—a point still debated in sociology and anthropology. Locke did not map a strategy for surmounting the antifunctionalist position, but he did, as in other instances, suggest that the assessment of cultural functionals can be objectively attained through the use of logic and reason. But we are brought back to an impasse, for, as in the case of many cultural comparatives, one person's reason and logic is another's emotion and bias.

Social Change and the Intellectuals

If cultures are steeped in tradition and chauvinism and if, as Locke suggested, the majority of people are common, how then can social change take place? Throughout his essays Locke looked to reason and rationality as the means of overcoming cultural bias and extreme subjectivity. He was *not* opposed to the fact that people have values, because he thought values necessary, but he was concerned with what *kind* of values they had. Locke suggested the need for a program that would reeducate so as to reconstruct certain cultural and value motifs. His reeducative process would entail study and training in analyses and interpretations of cultural values, beliefs, and ideologies.[27] This would be possible, according to Locke, because he viewed civilization and cultures as objective institutionalizations of their associated values, beliefs, and ideologies. Students would enter such a study armed with *normative principles* that would aid them in attitude and value formation. Locke's advocacy of normative principles does not contradict his stated idea of objectivity.

The *normative* states that to teach, one must *begin* with value assumptions and one must also have a idea of what one is teaching, and for what ends it is being taught. But even this normative orientation is viewed as relative by Locke. Thus education for social change would promote social change by promoting intercultural and intracultural relations. According to Locke, "relativistic normativism" would help "to achieve a better understanding of the nature of values and a greater openness to the values of other people

27. *Ibid.*, 206.

and other cultures without weakening their understanding and attachment to their own. It might help students to acquire a rational appreciation of reason, and at the same time not only of the function but of the nature of tradition and institutions and perhaps, to some degree, of mysticism and religion."[28] Such an education would promote what Locke called a "fixed and functional unity rather than a fixed and irrevocable one." He furthermore called for a revitalizing integration" in educational orientation. Locke was not very expansive in his use of revitalizing integration, but it can be conjectured that his revitalizing integration can also be applied to culture. For example, in a 1939 article, Locke refuted those who suggested that the cultural situation of blacks was analogous to the "nation within a nation" theory. "There is a majority fallacy . . . implying a situation of different culture levels or traditions, a system of cultural bulkheads, so to speak, each racially compartmentalized and water-tight."[29] Instead, Locke believed that "what is 'racial' for the American Negro resides merely in the overtones to certain fundamental elements of culture common to white and black and is his by adoption and acculturation . . . the subtle interpretation of the 'national' and the 'social' traits is interesting evidence of cultural cross-fertilization."[30] He also believed that "the cultural products of the Negro are distinctive hybrids; culturally 'mulatto' generations ahead of the mixed physical conditions and ultimate biological destiny, perhaps of the human stock."[31]

Locke was saying that cultural fusion or cultural cross-fertilization is important in cultural movements and cultural change. But whereas each culture is unique, Locke's point was that each may not be all *that* unique, since in multi-cultural societies, or better named, cultural pluralism, there is normally so much cultural give and take. It is recognition of this cultural exchange that enables different peoples or cultures possibly to move together toward some phase of integrative but pluralistic cultural life. Such a life denotes cultural

28. *Ibid.*, 208.
29. Alain Locke, "The Negro's Contribution to American Culture," *Journal of Negro Education*, VIII (July, 1939), 522.
30. *Ibid.*
31. *Ibid.*, 523.

fusion and mutual sharing, Locke's idea of cross-fertilization. Cultural fusion would indubitably cut away at the edges of cultural particulars and thus permit transcultural creations. This aspect of cultural sharing has always evoked the anger of creative blacks who view the pillage of many aspects of black culture by whites as one of the predicaments of black cultural life in the United States. Hence traditional adages in black cultural creation have been "you have to be one to know one" and "you have to have lived it to know it." Locke apparently rejected this view in his idea of cultural fusion and saw it as positive, even though he lamented the high price that black artistic and literary creators pay (in artistic resources and intellectual morale) for integration. As he stated it: "The Negro author is moving over more and more into the field of general authorship, while at the same time, the white author is moving ever more boldly and competently into the delineation of Negro life. Each of these trends is in itself as desirable as it was inevitable."[32]

Cultural cross-fertilization is only possible if individuals and groups from one culture can take on the role of the "cultural other." Such putting oneself in the skin and mind of the other refutes a strict sociology of knowledge which claims that each person or group "brings its own socio-cultural biases and traditions when viewing cultural themes and values." Consequently, we are all ultimately hemmed in by the familiar. Locke's culture plus other culture equals cultural synthesis suggests that we can (or at least *some* of us can) escape the relativist fallacy. Like the early Du Bois, Locke would posit cultural transformation as a special talent of the intellectuals. Locke believed that intellectuals, more than other members of the society, possess and can apply reason and logic in confronting social issues. It is they, he reasoned, who must help us to "discipline our thinking critically into some sort of realistic world-mindedness." Locke's universalist-minded intellectual can be compared to Du Bois' concept of the intellectual elite, in which Du Bois defined the intellectual as one who "ought to be the group leader, the man who sets the ideals of the community where he lives, di-

32. Alain Locke, "The High Price of Integration," *Phylon*, XIII (First Quarter, 1952), 7.

rects its thoughts and heads its social movements."[33] Hence, both Locke and Du Bois would pin their hope for cultural reconstruction and cultural pluralisms on intellectuals whose approach to knowledge and the social world is viewed as more amenable to pluralistic harmony.

Conclusion

Locke's importance in contemporary social thought rests upon his delineations in two substantive areas: his role as an explicator of Afro-American culture, and his role as an interpretator of the ideals of cultural pluralism and value relativism. With "The New Negro" essay, he became the chief interpreter of the thematic developments in black culture; in so doing he laid the foundation for new literary as well as sociological insights into the sense of social and racial awareness thought by many social thinkers to have reached a state of heightened development in the 1920s. Locke's response to this new awareness and sense of consciousness was not predicated on a simplistic Manichean-type dichotomy. Rather, he viewed this new Afro-American consciousness as an opportunity for blacks to do two things: deepen their cultural perspectives about the main features of black life and widen their cultural options and place the inner cultural world of blacks into a larger, more cosmopolitan setting. The cosmopolitan-parochial and relativist-pluralist debate meant, for Locke, zeroing in on two different areas: the cultural absolutism and value monism signified by the rise of nazism and fascism in Europe and the idea of the melting pot and Anglo-Saxon conformity in the United States. The policy of racial chauvinism, according to Locke, prompted the need for counternationalism by smaller racial and cultural groups, a nationalism that would lend credence to the group's sense of a collective self. Furthermore, Locke claimed, successful intergroup relations demand mutual interdependency and intergroup tolerance. Locke recognized that

33. Locke, "Pluralism and Intellectual Democracy," 208; Rutledge M. Dennis, "Du Bois and the Role of the Educated Elite," *Journal of Negro Education*, XLVI (Fall, 1977), 388; W. E. B. Du Bois, "The Talented Tenth," in Andrew Paschal (ed.), *A W. E. B. Du Bois Reader* (New York: Macmillan Books, 1971), 41.

cultural pluralism and the idea of value relativity remain mere ideals, that, in fact, cultural absolutism is more prevalent throughout the world. He also believed that this absolutism was one of the sources of the historic conflict between groups.

The chief value of Locke's works lies in his desire to paint a large rather than a thin, small picture of the nature of culture and values. Though primarily a philosopher, his desire to evoke historical, sociological, and anthropological insights into his analysis of group values stemmed from his vision that a holistic account can best contribute to our knowledge of a group's ethos. Locke raised some important questions for Afro-Americans. He understood the difficulty of biculturality but insisted that there is nothing inherently undesirable about it. Rather than viewing biculturality as an obstacle to a group's internal value consistency, he saw it as complementary and supplementary. For him value duality does not promote value confusion and need not promote wholesale personal or group cultural schizophrenia. On the surface, it would appear that Locke saw this "unity in diversity" as possible only for the few enlightened intellectuals. But he did not, even though he did think that intellectuals have a greater degree of tolerance toward cultural diversity and duality because of their intellectual training. He cautioned that extreme cultural and value chauvinism, because it promotes the idea of the superiority of one group over another, is bound to lead to totalitarianism, because the only way a group generally accepts another group's domination is through the existence of laws and military actions to keep the subordinate group in check. What Locke sought to promote was a new world that provided options for individuals and groups—that they would neither be forced to adhere to their historical cultural heritage nor be forced to convert to the cultural motifs of others. He believed that the choice of adhering to one or the other, both, or neither, is a choice that can be rationally and objectively made. For these reasons his ideas of pluralism and relativity remain just as potent for the 1970s and 1980s as they had been throughout the decades of the 1920s through the 1950s.

The Politics of Alain Locke

A. GILBERT BELLES

Recent investigations of Alain Locke are, if nothing else, contributing to a synthesis of a man whose traditional tags barely reflect the complexity of this individual whose interests were wide as well as deep. Locke was a professor of philosophy and a literary critic. He surveyed books by and about blacks and on music, drama, art, education, and Africa. He reviewed plays, musical productions, and art exhibits. Locke became a cultural spokesman in his thinking, writings, and actions, fusing a view of culture to its role in time and place and emphasizing the "artistic modes of knowing, feeling, and celebrating the life of man in society."[1]

But as many of his contemporaries observed, Locke was not unaware of the social, economic, and political sides of life. He had knowledge of, and spoke cogently about, the history and the politics of man in general and Americans and blacks in particular. Cultural recognition emerges as a top priority in one's scheme of life, but to Locke it could serve as a means to all sorts of ends. He did little prophesying, but he often tapped his resource of historical knowledge to comment upon contemporary black politics. In many respects Locke was an activist, more concerned with imme-

1. Richard A. Long, "Alain Locke: Cultural Mentor," in *Homage to Alain Locke: An Art Exhibition* (New York, 1970), 1.

50

diate events than most college teachers or intellectuals care to be. Some of his writing and activity can be categorized as political in nature, and this part of Locke's interests deserves separate attention.

Locke was a philosopher of the here and now, a thinker whose ideas were products of his time, place, and situation. His conclusions were not vague and aimless. His colleagues agreed that he was not an ivory tower recluse but a scholar-citizen who promoted his ideas and took strong positions either opposing or supporting the views of others. Locke was not an alarming presentist, but he was not above the battles of his own time and place. The storms of the nation's capital, the race riots, the discrimination failed to sweep up Locke in a maelstrom. But while he did not lose himself in these events, he did not turn away, did not hide as if in a cloister. Locke "asserted his belief that philosophers must deal with the daily problems that history produces."[2]

Locke used many forums to spread the truth, encourage youth, and disseminate his thoughts. For a start, as a college professor, he had Howard University to restructure. He introduced progressive reform into the curriculum, academic standards and a variety of graduation requirements into the degree, a department of drama into the program of arts and sciences, and an expanded library, art gallery, theater company, and literary magazine, *Stylus*. Campus politics provided a local setting for applying value judgments to daily activity. It was easier at this level to see that social, intellectual, academic, and political life were intimately related and that Locke could use culture as his ammunition for political battles.

These local activities did not detract from a wide range of interests that kept Locke busy as a professional philosopher, concerned citizen, and race-conscious Afro-American. He was a member of the American Philosophical Society and the American Ethnological Society. He was elected president of the American Association for Adult Education and founded the Associates in Negro Folk Education. Scholarly articles by Locke appeared in *Theater Arts, Musical*

2. Ernest Mason, "An Introduction to Alain Locke's Theory of Value" (Ph.D. dissertation, Emory University, 1975), 51.

Arts, and *Art in America.* Frequently he accepted temporary academic appointments at other universities, which enlarged his constituency of followers and protégés. He paid academic visits to the University of Wisconsin, the University of California, Sarah Lawrence College, the University of Chicago, Northwestern University, Syracuse University, and the New School of Social Research, and institutions in Haiti, Latin America, Africa, Paris, Rome, and Salzburg. His academic professionalism could not be questioned. And when called upon to teach war aims in the Officers' Training Camp on the Howard campus during World War I, Locke served. His civic duties also included a three-year stint as statistician for the New Jersey Semi-Centennial Commemoration of the Negro and a term as official observer for the Foreign Policy Association at the Geneva meeting of the League of Nations.

But even more interesting than his campus, professional, and civic activities were his actions, scholarly and political, in the interest of race, race culture, and race politics. As a young man Locke supported the Niagara Movement, Du Bois' faith in the Talented Tenth, and the attacks on the philosophies of Booker T. Washington. In 1924, Kelly Miller and Locke formed Sanhedrin, a national council to coordinate activity in race relations. Four years later Locke attended the National Interracial Conference in Washington, D.C., and reported it as the beginning of a crusade for social democracy. He played a major role in a conference at Howard University sponsored by the Phelps-Stokes Fund which featured South Africa's former prime minister Jan C. Smuts as guest. Locke pointed out there that more militant black Americans were formulating responses to injustices inherent in race questions pertaining to citizenship, housing, and education.[3]

Locke's interest in racial politics was not confined to attending and reporting about conferences. He wrote articles and essays on

3. Eugene Holmes, "The Legacy of Alain Locke," *Freedomways* (Summer, 1963), n.p.; Alain Locke, "The Negro Speaks for Himself," *Survey,* LII (April 15, 1924), 71; Alain Locke, "The Boxed Compass of Our Race Relations," *Southern Workman,* LVIII (February, 1929), 51–56; Alain Locke, "A Notable Conference," *Opportunity,* VIII (May, 1930), 137–40.

discrimination and race relations in *Crisis, Opportunity, Phylon, American Scholar, Progressive Education, Journal of Negro Education, Forum, Nation, Survey, Survey Graphic, Southern Workman,* and the *Encyclopaedia Britannica.* Locke was an active member of the American Negro Academy, the Association for the Study of Negro Life and History, and the International Institute of African Language and Culture.

This brief summary merely provides a quick glimpse into Locke's activities. He was a man who chose his words carefully and tried to make them count, and he stayed clear of emptiness and shallowness. His friends remember him as one who did not waste time nor engage in small talk. He attended, participated, observed, evaluated, and reported on the ongoing struggles that faced a college professor, a concerned citizen, and a freedom-conscious black American. In addition to Locke's activism, sufficient evidence can be adduced that he was a "political animal," a person whose political activism reflected a deep concern with immediate problems of discrimination and race relations. One can see this by turning to his essays and critiques, his own thoughts as expressed in original papers, and his opinions in reviews of major works pertaining to racial politics (as contrasted to works whose themes could be considered more literary, artistic, philosophical, or esoteric).

The remainder of this essay will concentrate on the statements by Locke that illustrate his political positions on social reform and realistic, practical change in American society or even the human condition. Locke's position reflected the tension, as he saw it, between the necessity for practical compromise on one side and the radical assertion of rights and principles on the other side—a tension often compared to that arising from the differences between Washington and Du Bois. And "although Locke called himself a pacifist and favored legal pressure through the courts, he was not so unhistorical minded or blinded to the limitations of legal action to see that physical force or violence may sometimes be necessary to help produce change."[4] One hastens to add that at no time did Locke ever favor

4. Mason, "An Introduction," 13.

physical violence as a tactic, nor did he even include it in his definitions of militancy. Militancy suggested to Locke an extreme position, and it was a label he fixed on some individuals; but in the context of his time, the term did not really imply street activity.

One of Locke's strategies was to use culture as ammunition in the battles for racial survival and progress. If blacks could be recognized as legitimate contributors to American and world culture, it followed that social proscriptions would be removed and the mood and creed of white supremacy would be scrapped. New political and social thinking and attitudes, linked to food, clothing, housing, and employment, would replace old accommodationist ideas among blacks and oppressive behavior among whites. Locke believed that he was in the tradition of other articulate blacks in American history who displayed strong racial consciousness as one way of fighting oppression. "He showed that . . . it was the anti-slavery movement which developed the intellect of the Negroes and pushed him [sic] forward to articulate, disciplined expression." In the 1920s, the Harlem Renaissance transformed blacks into "the New Negro, militant, no longer obsequious." [5]

One of Locke's colleagues, William Stanley Braithwaite, called Locke's 1925 book of essays, The New Negro, both a protest and an assumption—"a protest against the imposed limitations of the spirit of the Negro artist . . . and the assumption of his membership in the wide realm of human vision and imagination." [6] But even earlier than this seminal collection, Locke had formulated a stand on racial politics. In the second issue of Opportunity (February, 1923), Locke reviewed a play by Ernest Howard Culbertson titled Goat Alley: A Tragedy of Negro Life. The play turned out to be something less than promised, its intentions being greater than its achievements. Locke had expected "something more essentially racial." Dramas whose plot, motivation, and character had little that was peculiarly racial left "the race problem precisely where it stood or stands." [7] Black

5. Ibid., 69; Holmes, "The Legacy," n.p.
6. William Stanley Braithwaite, "Eulogy for Alain Locke," in Braithwaite folder, Cullen Jackman Collection, Atlanta University.
7. Alain Locke, "Goat Alley," a review of Ernest Howard Culbertson's Goat Alley: A Tragedy of Negro Life, in Opportunity, I (February, 1923), 30.

culture had a responsibility to provide enlightenment on the race problem and Locke panned work that failed to meet that criterion. In sharp contrast, just one year later in *Crisis*, Locke reviewed *There Is Confusion* by Jesse Fausett and found that "it throbs with some of the latest reactions of the race situation in this country upon the psychology and relations of colored and white Americans of the more intelligent classes."[8] Literary works that did this stood high on Locke's lists. In April, 1924, *Opportunity* carried Locke's review of *La Question des Noirs aux Etats-Unis* by Frank L. Schoell. This French author was praised, for his most brilliant chapter was an objective analysis of prejudice. Locke liked the directness with which white supremacy was presented, analyzed, and refuted. Schoell's faith in the principle of justice and the consistency of law and institutions as the most practical as well as the only right solution was justifiable, for it arose, as in this instance, from a really unpartisan analysis. In spite of his sympathy with the program of the theoretical protestants and with the position of the Negro intelligentsia, Schoell saw the question in the perspective of no single faction. His analysis of the various schools of thought was very clear and impartial. His estimate of the work of the National Association for the Advancement of Colored People and the National Urban League, as well as his interpretation of the significance of the Pan-African congresses, the Garvey movement, and other symptoms of rising race consciousness, was really a contribution to the analysis of the question.[9]

The mosaic of Locke's racial politics takes on another dimension with his critique of Edwin Mims's *The Advancing South*. He grants Mims "the cautiousness of tact rather than timidity" in his appraisal of the struggle for economic survival and social and educational reform in the South. Locke agreed that "the race problem cannot be isolated from the other social problems of the Southland. . . . Our best tactics for the future will be to join the common causes of pub-

8. W. E. B. Du Bois and Alain Locke, "The Younger Literary Movement," *Crisis*, XXVII (February, 1924), 163.

9. Alain Locke, "As Others See Us," a review of Frank L. Schoell's *La Question des Noirs aux Etats-Unis*, in *Opportunity*, II (April, 1924), 109.

lic enlightenment and welfare, to regard reactionism in politics, religion, and public thought as more, or at least as much as an enemy as race prejudice."[10]

Locke went on to compare the concept of a New South with that of the New Negro. He welcomed a New South, emancipated from old obsessions by new attitudes, leaders, philosophies, and policies. Class cooperation and mass education would raise the southern folk tradition to the level of accepted creative expression. And most important, the New South included a critical component: "The interracial movement, halting and cautious as it has been, is nevertheless full of fine potentialities—it is the only possible constructive basis of practical reform."[11] Locke was beginning to speak out on these racial issues in independent and original essays. These articles, together with his continuing assessments of other authors, provide the continuum of Locke's evolving beliefs about racial politics.

By the late 1920s, Locke advanced the position that America's problem was not "the Negro" but democracy itself and the predicament of an obsessed majority. Intelligent blacks should put forward "the common-sense practicalities of the concrete situation . . . [and] become the great critic[s] and challenging analyst[s] of our institutions." Black progress was in the hands of an intellectual elite whose first task was cultural development and recognition. For blacks it was necessary to reverse the standard order and not wait to reach the final stages of a leisure society before enjoying the fruits of success. Cultural contributions proved the humanity and equality of blacks. At this point, Locke's faith in the Talented Tenth dominated his strategy for change and progress. "I would so much prefer to see the black masses going gradually forward under the leadership of a recognized and representative and responsible elite than see a frustrated group of malcontents later hurl these masses at society in desperate strife."[12] Note also the willingness to proceed

10. Alain Locke, "Welcome the New South—A Review," *Opportunity*, IV (December, 1926), 374.
11. *Ibid.*, 375.
12. Alain Locke, "The High Cost of Prejudice," *Forum*, LXXVIII (December, 1927), 501, 507.

gradually. Later Locke abandoned and attacked what he called gradualism.

Locke saw validity in linking black progress to "new stirrings in the Negro mind and the dawning of new social objectives."[13] Artists and writers were not to perform the duties of reformers, but their use of racial material could awaken the consciousness of all Americans. And the problem was "not sectional but national . . . it cannot be either exclusively the white man's burden or the black man's burden, but is fundamentally interracial . . . it is neither exclusively educational, economic, nor political, but a composite."[14] He praised books like Edwin Embree's *Brown America*, because it had "the virtue of seeing the Negro as an integral part of democracy and its problems rather than as a special and separate problem. This integration of the Negro problem within the context of American life, economic, industrial, educational, political, is the pronounced trend."[15]

During the years of the Great Depression, Locke discerned a shift among black writers before he had articulated any new position of his own. Langston Hughes, called by Locke the chief exponent of the folk-school tradition, began "to turn more and more in the direction of social protest and propaganda . . . the poet of *Scottsboro, Ltd.* is a militant and indignant proletarian reformer."[16] Two years later, in 1935, Locke characterized Hughes's *The Ways of White Folks* as "the militant assault on the citadel of Nordicism in full fury, if not in full force. Avowedly propagandist, and motivated by radical social philosophy, we have here the beginnings of the revolutionary school of Negro fiction."[17] In this year, Locke titled his literary review in *Opportunity* the "Eleventh Hour of Nordicism," which to him meant the death knell for racist and white supremacist atti-

13. Alain Locke, "Beauty Instead of Ashes," *Nation*, CXXVI (April 18, 1928), 432.
14. Locke, "The Boxed Compass of Our Race Relations," 52.
15. Alain Locke, "We Turn to Prose," *Opportunity*, X (February, 1932), 41.
16. Alain Locke, "Black Truth and Black Beauty," *Opportunity*, XI (January, 1933), 17.
17. Alain Locke, "The Eleventh Hour of Nordicism, I," *Opportunity*, XIII (January, 1935), 10.

tudes. The most important dissenting influences against bland, innocuous, and inconsequential assertions about race relations came "from the militant but very rigorous scientific school of anthropologists captained by Professor [Franz] Boas. They have dared, in season and out, to challenge false doctrines and conventional myths, and were the first to bring the citadel of Nordicism into range of scientific encirclement and bombardment."[18]

At this point Locke began taking shots at certain theories of racial progress. The philanthropists and professional social workers concerned with interracial progress were dogmatically committed to "gradualism and good will . . . and that's that."[19] But James Weldon Johnson, in *Negro American, What Now?*, provided a commonsense analysis of the racial situation with favorable emphasis on the political and civil rights action of the NAACP. Locke viewed the political strategy of the NAACP as intelligent opportunism.

By the 1930s, Locke prepared an essay that offered legal adjudication as the best solution to ending the oppression of blacks. It was not a matter of alternatives but of expediency. Legal cases raised vague social grievances to the level of public wrongs. It was "worth the protest in the enhancement of self-respect alone, even if no practical results were to be obtained." Locke believed that the law seemed "to be one of the only resorts possible. Negroes, therefore, should and must resort to the courts to secure considerable or wholesale improvement of the situation." This article contained a strong attack on slower approaches. "Nothing is more contrary to fact than the rather wide-spread policy and program of gradualism. This theory of slow, accumulative growth, of the slow reform of public opinion, of 'the education of public sentiment,' is a fallacy. The lines of social reform are not smooth, gradual curves but jagged breaks, sudden advances, and inevitable setbacks of reaction."[20]

In another article that same year, 1935, Locke wrote that the

18. Alain Locke, "The Eleventh Hour of Nordicism, II," *Opportunity*, XIII (February, 1935), 46.
19. *Ibid.*, 47.
20. Alain Locke, "The Dilemma of Segregation," *Journal of Negro Education*, IV (July, 1935), 410, 407.

problems of cultural minorities in situations around the world made the racial conditions in America seem like "a precarious truce." He believed that "this ominous rainbow, with a few local but not significant variations, shows a wide diffusion of bias and prejudice in our social atmosphere and, unfortunately, presages not the passing, but the coming of a storm . . . and unless America solves these minority issues constructively and achieves minority peace or minority tolerance, in less than half a generation she will be in the flaming predicament of Europe." Locke charged the church with "talking mild platitudes" and the schools with remaining "strangely silent" on issues of widespread public concern. It was not the time for timorousness, temporizing, compromise, or apathy. Locke advocated that blacks "must build resistance to prejudiced and biased attitudes," and not merely by mouthing mild palliatives.[21]

Locke's reviews of other writing convinced him that black culture was "turning prosaic, partisan, and propagandist . . . in a protestant and belligerent universalism of social analysis and protest." While he hesitated to endorse the philosophy, he granted "the power, integrity, and increasing vogue of the Marxians."[22] Locke recognized that new fires burned, calling for a present-day social and economic reconstruction. Yet he could not "approve in full of Dr. Du Bois's passionate leap to close the gap and throw the discussion of the Negro problem to the forefront battleline of Marxian economics." He praised Charles S. Johnson's *Collapse of Cotton Tenancy* for its "scientific approach and mild militancy."[23]

Locke moved another step by 1937 when he surveyed the literature and found a wide variety of political opinions expressed. He took a poke at "the now professionalized gradualism of the missionaristic-philanthropic approach, which is the contemporary sur-

21. Alain Locke, "Minorities and the Social Mind," *Progressive Education*, XIII (March, 1935), 142.
22. Alain Locke, "Deep River: Deeper Sea, I," *Opportunity*, XIV (January, 1936), 7.
23. Alain Locke, "Deep River: Deeper Sea, II," *Opportunity*, XIV (February, 1936), 42.

vival of the Hampton-Tuskegee school of thought." Without vigorously endorsing it, Locke believed that "the class theory must be
credited at least with this fundamental gain,—that it . . . links the
Negro question into the general scheme and conditions of society."[24] Locke's loyalty to culture allowed him to find that "the
Negro literature of social protest has some distinctive qualities of
local color and idiom, quizzical irony, dashing satire, and freedom
from unrelieved drabness . . . the common factors of social re-
formism and relentless indictment are also there." In other words,
while Locke engaged in political dialogue, he maintained his cultural priorities. But he saw that "probably the next objective and
the next crusade in the ascending path of Negro art" was "its use as
an instrument for social enlightenment and constructive social reform." Locke believed that cultural politics influenced the entire social system and that there was an unavoidable tendency to use literature and art as political tools. In the case of black Americans, the
elusive goals of truth and beauty had been channeled off "by the
deepening disillusionment of the Negro's sad economic plight, into
a rising school of iconoclast protest fiction, poetry, and drama."[25]

It would be a distortion to call Locke a Marxian, but by 1940 he
heaped praise on the economic determinism of Charles S. Johnson
in *Race Relations and Social Change*. In this "admirable study" Johnson declared for "the economic factors as basically determining race
conflict issues." Moving out a little further on a limb, Locke credited the National Urban League with the discovery of the basic economic components of the race question. Looking back over its
thirty-year history, Locke recalled that the economic character of
racial politics was ignored by a majority of experts and leaders, but
the league focused on this problem. Further evidence of Locke's
awareness of black politics can be found in the *Britannica Year Book
1940*, where he discussed civil rights activity, court cases, protests,
labor unions, and farm tenant riots.[26]

One thing appears certain about Locke's evolving political con-

24. Alain Locke, "God Save Reality! II," *Opportunity*, XV (February, 1937), 40.
25. Alain Locke, "The Negro's Contribution to American Culture," *Journal of
Negro Education*, VIII (July, 1939), 527, 529.
26. Alain Locke, "Dry Fields and Green Pastures, II," *Opportunity*, XVIII (Febru-

sciousness. By the end of World War II his evaluation of the tension between practical compromise and radical assertion (Washington or Du Bois) resulted in his coming out for what he believed to be correct without qualification. His cyclic theory of the history of black progress had its militant phases, and in 1944 he wrote that "I myself (and I think in this I speak for a goodly section of Negro thinkers at this time) believe that we have made more substantial gains in the militant phases than in the others." Militance was "calculated to recover lost ground or gain fresh advances," and Locke found that the NAACP represented one form of militancy, that the Harlem Renaissance was cultural and social militancy, and that the New Deal was a phase of economic militancy. He believed reform and black progress reached another peak of militancy during World War II. The dirty laundry in America's backyard was now on the front porch of international relations. Democracy would have to pay for prejudice at some point, either by providing social justice now or by repairing the damage of social unrest later. Locke called for an immediate end to segregation as a first step toward ending the entrenched privileges that stained democracy in America.[27]

In 1942, he repeated a journalistic assignment for *Survey Graphic* and edited an entire issue reminiscent of "The New Negro." The newer issue, called "Color: The Unfinished Business of Democracy," put the politics of race relations on an international level. Two years later in the *Journal of Negro Education*, Locke diagrammed an elaborate political strategy for the improvement of race relations. His analysis concluded that race relations followed a typical course in United States history, including the current "acute protest stage of minority self assertion with its accompanying chauvinism." Locke contended that "we have come to a crisis where action and action alone can convince and count."[28]

ary, 1940), 44; Alain Locke, "A Contribution to American Culture," *Opportunity*, XXIII (Fall, 1945), 192; Alain Locke, "Negroes (American)," *Britannica Book of the Year 1940*, 485–86.

27. Alain Locke, "The Negro Group," in R. M. MacIver (ed.), *Group Relations and Group Antagonisms* (New York: Institute for Religious Studies, 1944), 47, 50.

28. Alain Locke, "Whither Race Relations? A Critical Commentary," *Journal of Negro Education*, XIII (Summer, 1944), 399, 401.

All of Locke's political positions and activities stood out in the memories of many of the friends who prepared eulogies at the time of his death. When they called him a scholar-citizen, they meant one who did not detach himself from daily practical issues. "He walked among the affairs of men with the eyes and the mind of an educated man." [29] Charles S. Johnson put it more strongly: "If his was a note of protest, it came clear and unquivering. But it was more than a protest note; it was one of social defiance which held behind it a spirit magnificent and glowing . . . a mood of stubborn defiance." [30] Very early in his own career, Locke provided a summary of his own political philosophy. "Let me assure you that I am not temperamentally of the sort that would bless the hand or the fate that had given me a stone for a pillow and a wilderness for a home. . . . I hope the faith of the elders can be retained without retaining of course their limitations of view and situation." [31] Locke's political visions and dreams were not impossible. They are an important if sometimes neglected aspect of this complex renaissance man.

29. "The Passing of Alain Leroy Locke," *Phylon*, XV (September, 1954), 243–52.
30. Charles S. Johnson, "The Negro Renaissance and Its Significance," in Rayford Logan, *et al.* (eds.), *The New Negro Thirty Years Afterward* (Washington, D.C.: Howard University Press, 1955), 80.
31. Alain Locke, "The Command of the Spirit," *Southern Workman*, LIV (July, 1925), 297.

Alain Locke, W. E. B. Du Bois and the Crisis of Black Education During the Great Depression

MANNING MARABLE

The most important, and perhaps least understood, period of W. E. B. Du Bois' intellectual life occurred during the years of the Great Depression. Moving sharply away from the National Association for the Advancement of Colored People, Du Bois advanced a program of rural consumer and producer cooperatives, self-segregation, and democratic socialism. In the field of education, Du Bois called for a new emphasis toward community involvement, racial integrity, and political militancy for black people. Consequently, Du Bois' published writings and speeches on black education were either attacked for returning to a Booker T. Washington-style of accommodation or condemned for their emphasis on socialist economics. Du Bois' single most important document of the decade, the Basic American Negro Creed, was a statement on these new themes within his thought. Accepted by Alain Locke and the American Association for Adult Education, the creed, though not published, represented the summation of Du Bois' frustrating search for a new approach to black liberation. The dialogue between Du Bois and Locke on the direction of black education represented an important chapter in the struggle toward an independent black strategy for social reconstruction in America.

By the outset of the depression, Du Bois had begun to doubt and thereafter seriously question his *raison d'être* within the segregation struggle. "My basic theory had been that race prejudice was primarily a matter of ignorance," he reflected later in *Dusk of Dawn*. "When the truth was properly presented, the monstrous wrong of race hate must melt and melt quickly before it." Certainly this faith in the inevitability of right was a by-product of the age of progressivism. The NAACP had succeeded in distributing literature in defense of Negro rights, had modified laws through litigation, and had changed the language of racial confrontation from crude racism to moderation. "Nevertheless," Du Bois stated, "the barriers of race prejudice were certainly as strong in 1930 as in 1910 the world over, and in certain aspects, from certain points of view, even stronger." It gradually occurred to Du Bois that "stronger and more threatening forces [formed] the founding stones of race antagonisms," rather than cultural hostility and emotionalism alone. He had been a moderate socialist for most of his adult life, and had always understood the economic imperatives behind the establishment of Jim Crow. Finally, in the wake of the Soviet revolution in 1917, Du Bois turned little by little to Marxism for a more comprehensive analysis of the economic origins of racism.[1]

Realistically, Du Bois faced the somber prospect of a world in which racial prejudice was a permanent feature, a cultural expression of class exploitation of black people. "Slowly but surely I came to see that for many years, perhaps many generations," racial equality would be an illusion rather than a reality. "Therefore, I began to emphasize and restate certain implicit aspects of my former ideas." Du Bois urged blacks to work together in separate economic, cultural, and political institutions. Black Americans had to become more conscious of the national strivings of black people throughout the diaspora. "This plan did not establish a new segregation," Du Bois noted; "it did not advocate segregation as the final solution of the race problem." However, many if not all of Du Bois' oldest supporters were shocked and deeply disturbed by the new national-

1. W. E. B. Du Bois, *Dusk of Dawn: An Essay Toward an Autobiography of a Race Concept* (New York: Harcourt Brace, 1940), 282–84.

ist directions that the *Crisis* editor was advocating. Du Bois recognized that the "matter of segregation" was "an old and bleeding sore in Negro thought. . . . The upper class Negro has almost never been nationalistic." Du Bois was adamant, though, that his program of deliberate segregation in the development of black America must eventually "increase the Negro's acceptability to white Americans."[2]

Mordecai Johnson, Howard University's new president, invited Du Bois to deliver the commencement address at the university in June, 1930. Du Bois' initial response to Johnson, dated March 4, 1930, reveals the considerable revision of his past views on black education. Du Bois reflected that for over a generation the Hampton-Tuskegee model of industrial education had been in bitter conflict with his own beliefs, which "called for an education that transcended and went far beyond technical training for manual labor." The black leader commented sadly that "both sides of this controversy" had failed in their educational pursuits. "Industrial education has not produced any great number of farmers and artisans among American Negroes, and, on the other hand, college training is sending a disproportionate number of our trained men into the learned professions." Negro education lacked direction and purpose, Du Bois suggested, because it was not tied into a practical program for social transformation. The immense economic sufferings of the Depression had forced Du Bois to refine his elitist Talented Tenth formula for Negro education in favor of a more specific agenda for economic reform at a mass level. "To train men for art, literature and thought," Du Bois admitted, "and to leave the necessary technicality of manual toil to be done by ignorant people, is to undermine the basis of civilization and to work straight toward caste and slavery."[3]

In his Howard University address, Du Bois argued that most black colleges "have [not] yet comprehended the age in which they

2. *Ibid.*, 306–308.
3. W. E. B. Du Bois to Mordecai Johnson, March 4, 1930, in Herbert Aptheker (ed.), *The Correspondence of W. E. B. Du Bois* (2 vols.; Amherst: University of Massachusetts Press, 1973, 1976), I, 420–21.

live: the tremendous organization of industry, commerce, capital, and credit which today forms a superorganization dominating and ruling the universe, subordinating to its ends government, democracy, religion [and] education." Du Bois believed that there was a sore lack of direction within the average administrations of black colleges, an unwillingness to break from bourgeois illusions and traditions. "The average Negro undergraduate has swallowed hook, line, and sinker, the dead bait of the white undergraduate who . . . does not think." Du Bois called for a unity of the two divided ideals of industrial and higher education in an effort to combat the "growing mass of stupidity and indifference" at Howard, Fisk, and other Negro colleges.[4]

As the depression grew worse, Du Bois moved ever more closely toward a separatist approach concerning black education and culture. At Fisk University's 1933 commencement, Du Bois presented his new views in his speech, "The Field and Function of the Negro College." Briefly, Du Bois explained to his audience that there was a basic difference between education and black education. "No matter how much we may dislike the statement, the American Negro problem is and must be the center of the Negro university. It has got to be." Du Bois broke with the idea that higher education should be nonracial in character. "There is no use pretending that you are . . . teaching white Americans," he stated succinctly. The sole purpose of the Negro college "must be grounded in the condition and work of black men!" The black college, unlike white institutions, should seek "to reach modern science of matter and life from the surroundings and habits and aptitudes of American Negroes and thus lead up to understanding of life and matter in the universe." Specifically, Du Bois argued that all black thought should be directed to serve the pressing material needs of black people. Culturally, black literature should reflect the historic and aesthetic values of Afro-Americans. Du Bois asked:

> Why was it that the Renaissance of literature which began among Negroes ten years ago has never taken real and lasting root? It

4. W. E. B. Du Bois, "Education and Work," in Herbert Aptheker (ed.), *The Education of Black People* (Amherst: University of Massachusetts Press, 1973), 66–67.

was because it was a transplanted and exotic thing. It was a literature written for the benefit of white people and at the behest of white readers, and starting out primarily from the white point of view. It never had a real Negro constituency and it did not grow out of the inmost heart and frank experience of Negroes; on such an artificial basis no real literature can grow. On the other hand, if starting in a great Negro university you have knowledge, beginning with the particular, and going out to universal comprehension and unhampered expression, you are going to begin to realize for the American Negro the full life which is denied to him now.[5]

These ideas were responsible in part for Du Bois' split with the board of directors of the NAACP and its executive secretary, Walter White. Du Bois resigned from the NAACP in the summer of 1934.

During this period of transition in Du Bois' own educational philosophy, he maintained a close, although occasionally uneven, relationship with Alain Locke, Howard University professor of philosophy and central spokesman for the Negro renaissance in literature. When Howard University's board of trustees curtly dismissed Locke and three other professors in 1927, Du Bois protested immediately to Howard trustee Jesse Edward Moorland, the treasurer of the Association for the Study of Negro Life and History. Du Bois explained to Moorland that Locke was not a particularly close friend and that he had not always agreed with him. Nevertheless, Du Bois insisted that Locke's rude dismissal amounted to the surrender of "the privilege of free speech and independent thinking" at Howard. Du Bois believed that the university would discourage young black scholars from seeking employment there if Locke were not permitted to remain. "Locke is by long odds the best trained man among the younger American Negroes," he wrote. "His place . . . ought to be at the largest Negro college, Howard." Locke was eventually rehired, but discontent among the major protagonists remained. The essence of the problem, as Du Bois viewed it, was a lack of freedom and political direction within all black education.[6]

5. Ibid., 92–93, 95, 96.
6. W. E. B. Du Bois to Jesse E. Moorland, May 5, 1927, Moorland to Du Bois,

Du Bois' correspondence indicates an ambiguous relationship with Locke in the context of the latter's educational views. For example, in November, 1925, economist Abram L. Harris, Jr., then serving as executive secretary for the Minneapolis Urban League, wrote to Du Bois and suggested that "a general shake-up was needed . . . throughout the entire realm of Negro education." Harris advanced the establishment of an all-black "Newer Spirit College," and suggested that Alain Locke would perhaps be interested in it. Du Bois responded cautiously, "wish[ing] we could have somewhere in the north, an institution which would be a center of Negro culture and learning [employing] an unshackled faculty of men of real education and untrammeled ideals." In 1933, Harris proposed to Du Bois the creation of a black speaker's bureau whose lecturers would talk at Negro colleges in an effort to promote social change. Du Bois endorsed the idea; possible lecturers included Charles H. Wesley, Rayford Logan, Ernest Just, E. Franklin Frazier, Sterling Brown, Charles Johnson, and Locke as potential participants. "At present," Du Bois declared, "our talent is being strangled to death and there is no more tremendous proof of the Marxian dogma than the fact that our fundamental economic situation today is making science, art and literature among us almost impossible." Du Bois had become convinced, unlike Locke, that the chief object of black education should be "action toward economic salvation."[7]

Locke's approach to the problem of race was significantly different from Du Bois'. Trained as a philosopher, Locke attempted to provide a philosophical rationalization for a New Negro culture

---

May 12, 1927, in Aptheker (ed.), *Correspondence of W. E. B. Du Bois*, I, 352–53. Du Bois had been largely responsible for the firing of the white president at Fisk University during a period of student unrest several years before. Du Bois considered the "turmoil at Howard" and the "uprising at Fisk" to have been both part of the same crisis in black education. "The struggle was epochmaking. How far can a Negro college, dominated by white trustees and a white president and supported by white wealth, carry on in defiance of the wishes and best interests of its colored constituency?" *Dusk of Dawn*, 282.

7. Abram L. Harris, Jr., to W. E. B. Du Bois, November 21, 1925, Du Bois to Harris, December 15, 1925, Du Bois to Harris, January 3, 1934, all in Aptheker (ed.), *Correspondence of W. E. B. Du Bois*, I, 327–28, 470–71.

that differed sharply from those cultural experiences of the so-called folk Negro. Locke argued in 1923 that race had no direct relationship with culture. "There is the general presumption and feeling that they have some quite vital and relevant connection," Locke noted, adding that this view was erroneous. "It will be our contention that far from being constants, these important aspects of human society are variables, and in the majority of instances not even paired variables." Locke criticized the natural scientific and anthropological definitions of race as incomplete and overgeneralized, especially in the light of recent scholarship. "The best consensus of opinion then seems to be that race is a fact in the social and ethnic sense [and not] in the physical sense." He implied that culture was a fusion of ethnic strains and reciprocal influences, whereas race "operates as tradition, as preferred traits and values." The literature of the New Negro was dialectical in a Hegelian sense, continually moving from the narrow boundaries of its racial origins toward the "deeper sea" of cultural reciprocity and universality. Locke insisted that cultural assimilation and development, rather than a reinforcement of racial distinctiveness and separation, were the keys for ultimate aesthetic beauty and humanism.[8]

Like Du Bois in an earlier period, Locke championed the development of a black intelligentsia, the Talented Tenth, as a critical part of black education. The modern challenge to education, Locke observed in 1918, was the education of a new democratic leadership class. "The future belongs to that class who can best grasp and embrace it." Locke insisted that higher education had to incorporate new intellectual and cultural values to prepare students for the changing political realities of the postwar period. "Patriotism, race policies and traditions, ideals of success, and even of culture must all undergo more or less fundamental revision, or we shall be bringing an old moral order to the gauging of a new social order, and err in consequence." Significantly, Locke's insistence that education be placed "upon a broader cultural basis" did not include an analysis of industrial or agricultural training institutions, the

8. Alain Locke, "The Concept of Race as Applied to Social Culture," *Howard Review*, I (1924), 290–99.

schools most black youth attended. Locke viewed the problem of cultural and social transformation in strictly elitist terms; black intellectuals, not the black masses, would initiate all humanistic and educational challenges against the white establishment. The fundamental concern of Locke was whether the proper leadership was "in the saddle." If so, he believed "the race is won."[9]

Locke planned a series of lectures entitled "Problems, Programs and Philosophies of Minority Groups," which was scheduled at Howard University in April, 1935. He had invited a number of influential liberal and leftist intellectuals, including Otto Klineberg of Columbia University, William Ernest Hocking of Harvard University, Sidney Hook, Ralph Bunche, E. Franklin Frazier, and Abram Harris of Howard University. Locke requested in his correspondence of March 15 that Du Bois take the topic "Negro Group Alternatives Today." Du Bois received the letter in late March while attending a black economic conference at Prairie View College in Texas. He accepted and returned to Washington, D.C., in time to deliver a successful presentation on April 6.[10]

While in Washington, D.C., Locke had informally discussed with Du Bois the possibility of his contribution to a series of booklets on education. Funded by the Carnegie Corporation through the American Association for Adult Education, the Adult Education Series was designed to examine various perspectives on black American economic, cultural, and historical development. Initially, nine booklets were to be published: two by Locke, "The Art of the Negro" and "The Negro and His Music"; two on literature and drama, by Sterling Brown; "The Economic Side of the Race Question" by Abram Harris; "World Aspects of the Race Problem" by Ralph Bunche; one on adult education, by Eugene K. Jones; "An Outline on Negro History" by Carter G. Woodson; and "Social Reconstruction and the Negro" by Du Bois. Recently Du Bois had completed his magnum opus, *Black Reconstruction*, and perhaps

9. Alain Locke, "The Role of the Talented Tenth," *Howard University Record*, XII (December, 1918), 15–18.
10. Alain Locke to W. E. B. Du Bois, March 15, 1935, Du Bois to Locke, March 23, 1935, in Aptheker (ed.), *Correspondence of W. E. B. Du Bois*, II, 77–79.

viewed Locke's invitation as a method of exploring contemporary economic problems in regard to racial development that might lead to a "Second Reconstruction." Returning to Atlanta, Du Bois agreed to complete the booklet before the summer. His only suggestion, which Locke immediately accepted, was a change in title, to "The Negro and Social Reconstruction." Du Bois explained simply, "It makes a slight difference in the point of view."[11]

The brief essay sharply criticized the approaches of the New Deal in regard to black economic and social development and suggested remedies that called for a socialization of the private market economy. Du Bois repudiated the NAACP ideal of integration in favor of a segregated plan of action in which blacks would organize all educational, economic, and cultural institutions as separately as possible from the larger white society. Significantly, the essay included Du Bois' Basic American Negro Creed, a brief statement of principles advocating socialism, racial pride and unity, full employment, black workers' councils, and the equalization of public wealth through progressive taxation.

Despite its importance, the Basic American Negro Creed is not widely known, and it is frequently difficult even to find a copy of it. Even a brief examination of its text will show the gulf that separated Du Bois from Locke over the issues involved. Said Du Bois:

1. We American Negroes are threatened today with lack of opportunity to work according to gifts and training and lack of income sufficient to support healthy families according to standards demanded by modern culture.

2. In industry, we are a labor reservoir, fitfully employed and paid a wage below subsistence; in agriculture, we are largely disfranchised peons; in public education, we tend to be disinherited illiterates; in higher education, we are the parasites of reluctant and hesitant philanthropy.

3. In the current reorganization of industry, there is no adequate effort to secure us a place in industry, to open opportunity for Negro ability, or to give us security in age or unemployment.

11. W. E. B. Du Bois to Alain Locke, March 23, 1935, Locke to Du Bois, April 17, 1935, Du Bois to Locke, April 26, 1935, Locke to Du Bois, April 29, 1935, Du Bois to Locke, May 16, 1935, ibid., 79–81.

4. Not by the development of upper classes anxious to exploit the workers, nor by the escape of individual genius into the white world, can we effect the salvation of our group in America. And the salvation of this group carries with it the emancipation not only of the darker races of men who make the vast majority of mankind, but of all men of all races. We therefore, propose this:

BASIC AMERICAN NEGRO CREED

A. As American Negroes, we believe in unity of racial effort, so far as this is necessary for self-defense and self-expression, leading ultimately to the goal of a united humanity and the abolition of all racial distinctions.

B. We repudiate all artificial and hate-engendering deification of race separation as such; but just as sternly, we repudiate an enervating philosophy of Negro escape into an artificially privileged white race which has long sought to enslave, exploit and tyrannize over all mankind.

C. We believe that the Talented Tenth among American Negroes, fitted by education and character to think and do, should find primary employment in determining by study and measurement the present field and demand for racial action and method by which the masses may be guided along this path.

D. We believe that the problems which now call for such racial planning are Employment, Education and Health; these three: but the greatest of these is employment.

E. We believe that the labor force and intelligence of twelve million people is more than sufficient to supply their own wants and make their advancement secure. Therefore, we believe that, if carefully and intelligently planned, a cooperative Negro industrial system in America can be established in the midst of and in conjunction with the surrounding national industrial organization and in intelligent accord with that reconstruction of the economic basis of the nation which must sooner or later be accomplished.

F. We believe that Negro workers should join the labor movement and affiliate with such trade unions as welcome them and treat them fairly. We believe that Workers' Councils organized by Negroes for interracial understanding should strive to fight race prejudice in the working class.

G. We believe in the ultimate triumph of some form of Socialism the world over, that is, common ownership and control of the means of production and equality of income.

H. We do not believe in lynching as a cure for crime; nor in war as a necessary defense of culture; nor in violence as the only path to economic revolution. Whatever may have been true in other times and places, we believe that today in America we can abolish poverty by reason and the intelligent use of the ballot, and above all by that dynamic discipline of soul and sacrifice of comfort which, revolution or no revolution, must ever be the only real path to economic justice and world peace.

I. We conceive this matter of work and equality of adequate income as not the end of our effort, but the beginning of the rise of the Negro race in this land and the world over, in power, learning and accomplishment.

J. We believe in the use of our voice for equalizing wealth through taxation, for vesting the ultimate power of the state in the hands of the workers; and as an integral part of the working class, we demand our proportionate share in administration and public expenditure.

K This is and is designed to be a program of racial effort and this narrowed goal is forced upon us today by the unyielding determination of the mass of the white race to enslave, exploit and insult Negroes; but to this vision of work, organization and service, we welcome all men of all colors so long as their subscription to this basic creed is sincere and is proven by their deeds.[12]

Du Bois completed "The Negro and Social Reconstruction" by the last week of May, 1935, and forwarded the manuscript to Locke immediately. Locke replied on June 4 that "at cursory glance it looks very interesting and adequate." Locke wrote that he would forward forty dollars to cover secretarial fees and one hundred dollars for honorarium. Another hundred would be "payable on completion of editorial correction and proofreading by the author." For over one year Du Bois heard nothing about the Adult Education Series. On June 27, 1935, he wrote to Locke that he had not received his initial honorarium. By February, 1936, Du Bois com-

12. Du Bois, *Dusk of Dawn*, 320–21.

plained, "My dear Mr. Locke: What on earth has become of our booklets?" After several more letters, Locke finally wrote Du Bois in March, 1936. "You are certainly entitled to an explanation as to why you haven't heard from me," he apologized. "At present, the only [manuscript] in hand is yours and one of my own." Later Locke explained, "I quite sympathized with your inquiry and your legitimate impatience about the booklets. But we are dealing with 'our kin folk,' and you ought to know them." All of the booklets had to be printed simultaneously to save expenses. After several more months, Du Bois' manuscript was at last edited for publication.[13]

Du Bois may have suspected finally that his essay was entirely too controversial for the Carnegie Corporation to publish and that this was the real reason for the delay. If so, his worst fears were soon confirmed by Alain Locke. On May 30, 1936, Locke informed Du Bois that he was "of the opinion that it would be unwise to print the basic American Negro Creed. . . . I can scarcely see how we could steer [clear] in that case of criticism on grounds of direct propaganda." Locke enclosed a check for one hundred dollars to Du Bois, adding, "I find myself in complete agreement" with the remainder of the booklet. "[I] can assure you that the [manuscript] will be printed substantially as is." Six months later, while Du Bois was on a world tour, Locke wrote to Du Bois' Atlanta office. "It was decided that it would be inadvisable to publish your manuscript, 'Social Reconstruction and the Negro,' largely because of its frequent references to specific situations of public program and policy." Locke added that the committee did not believe that even an extensive revision would "make this manuscript appropriate for publication now."[14]

There are several possible reasons why "The Negro and Social

13. Du Bois to Locke, May 28, 1935, Locke to Du Bois, June 4, 1935, Du Bois to Locke, February 27, 1936, Locke to Du Bois, undated, probably early March, 1936, Locke to Du Bois, March 6, 1936, Du Bois to Locke, May 22, 1936, in Aptheker (ed.), *Correspondence of W. E. B. Du Bois*, II, 81–84.

14. Locke to Du Bois, May 30, 1936, Locke to Du Bois, November 30, 1936, *Ibid.*, 84–85.

Reconstruction" remained unpublished. One of the contributors to the Adult Education Series, E. Franklin Frazier, had written a stinging critique of Du Bois' new prosegregationist ideas in the leftist journal, *Race*. Frazier, George Streator, Henry Lee Moon, and other young black intellectuals believed that Du Bois' advocacy of self-segregation and all-black cooperatives was simply a return to Booker T. Washington-style economics. Frazier had also privately criticized Du Bois' proposed *Encyclopedia of the Negro*. Carter G. Woodson, another proposed contributor to the series, used the pages of the Baltimore *Afro-American* to condemn the project.[15] To many older scholars like Locke, Du Bois seemed perhaps too far to the left and too nationalistic. Without his position as editor of the *Crisis*, Du Bois lacked the moral and intellectual authority he once held over both white liberals and the Negro intelligentsia. His Basic American Negro Creed seemed to repudiate the many years of activism in behalf of an integrationist perspective in Negro education.

Herbert Aptheker, Du Bois' biographer, suggested that the essay was never published "perhaps because it was highly critical of the New Deal." Locke avoided making negative comments about the New Deal administration of Franklin Roosevelt and supported particularly those programs that had cultural overtones. The contribution of Abram Harris, the "young Turk" who sympathized with Du Bois, was replaced in favor of "The Negro and Economic Reconstruction" by T. Arnold Hill of the Urban League. In *Dusk of Dawn*, Du Bois reflected that the study "proved unacceptable both to the Adult Education Association and to its colored affiliates. Consequently when I returned from abroad the manuscript, although ordered and already paid for, was returned to me as rejected

15. Frazier's relations with Du Bois mellowed with the passage of time. Frazier to Du Bois, May 11, 1944, Du Bois to Frazier, May 15, 1944, in Aptheker (ed.), *Correspondence of W. E. B. Du Bois*, II, 399–400. Also see Du Bois, *The Autobiography of W. E. B. Du Bois* (New York: International Publishers, 1968), 346, 368, 396. Woodson tended to idealize the self-help educational program of Tuskegee and deplored the lack of "race consciousness" evident within many of Du Bois' own followers. Du Bois' concept of the Talented Tenth seemed to Woodson both idealistic and elitist in the extreme. See Carter G. Woodson, *Miseducation of the Negro* (Washington, D.C.: Associated Publishers, 1933), 57.

for publication." Du Bois did not openly criticize Locke's role in the incident. "Just who pronounced the veto," he stated characteristically, "I do not know."[16]

The writing of W. E. B. Du Bois moved through three distinct yet overlapping phases: the period of integration, from the late 1890s to the mid 1920s; the period of democratic socialism and separatism, from the late 1920s to the mid 1940s; the period of Marxism-Leninism, from the late 1940s to 1963. In each period, Du Bois attempted earnestly to relate his intellectual work to the practice of challenging and changing white racist America.[17] Especially in the field of education, Du Bois' concern for black liberation assumes critical importance. For our historical period, Du Bois' middle period writing on education is especially instructive. He attempted in both his personal correspondence and in his published writings to rethink his former crusade for integration in the light of the perseverance of white racism. Du Bois' advocacy of self-segregation as a legitimate avenue for racial development within the framework of a mature capitalist society still promises to be perhaps the most important element of his intellectual legacy in our time.

16. Aptheker (ed.), *The Correspondence of W. E. B. Du Bois*, II, 58; Du Bois, *Dusk of Dawn*, 322.

17. This does not suggest by any means he did not exhibit nationalistic tendencies quite early in his intellectual career, nor does he ever quite abandon his Talented Tenth schema. Du Bois himself never considered his new turn toward self-segregation as black nationalism. Du Bois' turn toward the Communist party during the 1950s was in a sense the culmination of a series of ideas and events dating back to 1911, when he initially joined the Socialist party. However, during the 1930s and early 1940s, Du Bois concentrated more closely on the validity of a separatist economic and cultural solution for Afro-American development than at any other time.

Toward an Aesthetic of Black Folk Expression

REBECCA T. CUREAU

I

The New Negro was not a sudden metamorphosis but was the product of gradual change. Of all the forces at work in the shaping of the first two decades of the twentieth century, the movement toward black selfhood, an outgrowth of black nationalism, was perhaps the most significant for Negro Americans. The question no longer was "Who am I?" but was now "How shall I express who I am?" The shift from the first question to the second was significant. The intense literary and artistic activity involved in the new emphasis came to be known as the Negro renaissance, or the New Negro movement.[1]

Three of the individuals who gave significant direction to the New Negro movement were Alain Leroy Locke, W. E. B. Du Bois, and James Weldon Johnson. Of the three, Alain Locke was the most direct catalyst, and he is credited with describing the movement as a renaissance.[2] According to Eugene Holmes, "as a critic, philosopher, and teacher, Locke did more to shape the atti-

1. See Jean Wagner, *Black Poets of the United States* (Urbana: University of Illinois Press, 1973), 150*n.*
2. Derived from the title of an article by Alain Locke, "Our Little Renaissance," in Charles S. Johnson (ed.), *Ebony and Topaz* (New York: Association for the Study of Negro Life and History, 1927), 117–18.

tude and thinking of a generation of Negro youth than any other educator of his time, reflecting, as he did, a critical insight and cultural sensitivity that has not been surpassed."[3] Pleased because younger artists had found beauty in themselves, "in their instinctive love and pride of race," he looked to them to help advance the race and to bring about a favorable reevaluation of the Negro by white America. The "saving grace of realism," however, would, in the 1930s, cause him to advise Negro writers to be more universally relevant, to look beyond the narrow field of Negro life for more relevant answers to basic problems. But in asking artists to be universally relevant, he was not suggesting that they drop their racial perspective but rather that they merely blend the two together. His earlier renaissance goals of truth and beauty continued to be paramount, and he wrote that "in the end we shall achieve the promise that was so inspiring in the first flush of the Negro awakening,—a black beauty that is truth—a Negro truth that is purely art."[4]

A pioneer sociologist, historian, and creative artist, W. E. B. Du Bois published in 1903 *The Souls of Black Folk*, a group of essays dealing primarily with America's treatment of Negroes. This work was to set the scene for a new kind of informed and uncompromising leadership. Du Bois had a strong sense of race pride and saw great value in drawing upon the racial heritage. He was an early advocate of the use of black folk music for a classical American music tradition. Though he felt that art and propaganda could not be separated, he took the middle-class position that characterization of black life should project a proper image of the Negro.

James Weldon Johnson, an educator, song writer, poet, novelist, and diplomat, may be properly regarded as one of America's best known and most respected black leaders. Like Locke, Johnson wanted black artists to strive for the universal in their art, believing they would best interpret universal themes by dramatizing their ra-

---

3. Eugene Holmes, "Alain Locke—Philosopher, Critic, Spokesman," *Journal of Philosophy*, LIV (February 28, 1957), 113–18.
4. Alain Locke, "Black Truth and Black Beauty," *Opportunity*, XI (January, 1933), 14–18.

cial experience, "since race perforce was the thing the American Negro artist knew best." During the 1920s Johnson was the most important voice supporting the artistic exploration of the Negro's folk heritage.[5]

While each of these leaders in some way had a direct bearing on the New Negro renaissance, it is important to take note of the manner in which their approaches to the interpretation of the cultural heritage differed. It is perhaps in the points at which their philosophies differed that one senses a movement in the direction of the development of a black aesthetic, or an aesthetic of black art. Whether conscious or unconscious, these differences were of consequence to how the members of the Harlem Renaissance regarded their own work as well as each other's efforts. It was important also in regard to how the "audience"—both black and white—judged, criticized, and assessed the work of the young Harlem artists.

II

Writing in the April, 1915, issue of *Crisis*, Du Bois said: "In art and literature we should try to loose the tremendous emotional wealth of the Negro and the dramatic strength of his problems through writing . . . and other forms of art. We should resurrect forgotten ancient Negro art and history, and we should set the black man before the world as both a creative artist and a strong subject for artistic treatment." Seven years later J. W. Johnson wrote, "There is only one measure by which the greatness of a people can be recognized . . . and that is the amount and standard of literature and art they have produced."[6]

Thus, in subtly different ways, Du Bois and Johnson stated what were to be recurrent themes of the decade of the twenties: the Negro as producer and subject of art, and the Negro's artistic output as indices of his contribution to American life. Agreeing with

5. James O. Young, *Black Writers of the Thirties* (Baton Rouge: Louisiana State University Press, 1973), 151.
6. Arthur P. Davis, *From the Dark Tower* (Washington, D.C.: Howard University Press, 1974), 18, 27.

Du Bois' position, Locke was later to identify this race "genius" as a "vast spiritual endowment from which our best developments have come and must come." But of equal concern to Locke was the fact that he sensed in "the latest phases of social change and progress" a New Negro that was more in the "internal world of the Negro mind and spirit."[7] This New Negro wished "to reveal through self-portraiture his essential traits, in the full perspective of his achievements and possibilities." Much had been written *about* the Old Negro; the New Negro wished to speak for himself.

The younger Negroes felt great pride in their race and felt no need to be ashamed of those characteristics that made them seem different. In Locke's view, race for the younger generation was "but an idiom of experience, a sort of added enriching adventure and discipline, giving subtler overtones to life, making it more beautiful and interesting." The newer motive for being racial, Locke contended, "was purely for the sake of art." He saw an "increasing tendency to evolve from racial substance something technically distinctive, something that as an idiom of style may become a contribution to the general resources of art." To the younger artists, who, having achieved an inner mastery of mood and spirit, had come the "happy release from self-conscious rhetoric, bombast, and the hampering habit of setting artistic values with primary regard for moral effect." That habit he regarded as "pathetic overcompensation of a group inferiority complex which our social dilemmas inflicted upon several unhappy generations."[8]

It is perhaps on this latter point that disagreement between Locke and Du Bois may be most apparent. Du Bois' militant thinking led him to the conclusion that "all art is propaganda, and ever must be. . . . I stand in utter shamelessness and say that whatever art I have for writing has been used always for propaganda." Opposed

---

7. Alain Locke, "The New Negro," in Locke (ed.), *The New Negro* (New York: Arno Press, 1968), 49. Locke observes that in the younger generation of Negro writers and artists he sees both "a new aesthetic and a new philosophy of life." This seems to suggest that he views this as an indication of an evolving aesthetic of black art.

8. *Ibid.*, 46, 51.

to this position, Locke wrote in his article "Art or Propaganda" that "art in the best sense is rooted in self-expression and whether naive or sophisticated is self-contained. In our spiritual growth, genius and talent must more and more choose the role of group expression, or even, at times the role of free individualistic expression, — in a word must choose art and put aside propaganda."[9] There was no disagreement, however, that the Negro's culture and his racial heritage was the subject matter best suited for portrayal of the Negro.

III

But for all his new self-assertion, the Negro's gradual development into artistic selfhood, Locke felt, lay in the recovery of his cultural past, with its African backgrounds rooted in the plantation culture of the South. In reaching back to this source, black artists were showing willingness and ability to transform the richness and diversity, the intensity and anguish of the black American experience into the materials of art and literature. The folk heritage of the Negro was an important reservoir from which to draw for creative expression. This attempt by Locke, Du Bois, Johnson, and others of the Harlem movement to identify strengths and potentialities in folk culture as the basis for a black American tradition of literature and art bear striking similarity to the folk ideology of Johann Herder, the German philosopher, writer, and folklorist. As a philosopher, with his own well-stated position on cultural pluralism, Locke, one would assume, was well read in various theories of folk culture. All three, no doubt, were familiar with Anglo-Americans' interpretations of Herder's theory that folk art laid the base for higher art and with his concept of folk song as the spontaneous expression of the collective people, the latter concept being a frequent reference of Locke and Du Bois in regard to spirituals. Stirred by the vitality of Afro-American folk song and in their search for a new phase of group development, it is quite likely that these leaders of the New Negro movement saw great potential for the creative

9. Wagner, *Black Poets of the United States*, 170; Alain Locke, "Art or Propaganda?" *Harlem*, I (November, 1928), 12.

applications of the implications of Herder's theories to the spirituals, sermons, blues, and jazz.[10]

The inheritance of Negro folklore from its African backgrounds makes it distinct from other regional folk traditions of the New World; without its African antecedents there would be no unique Negro folklore. Many contend that the rich and complex folklore and music of the Afro-American is the most distinctly American contribution to world culture, and America's only genuine folk tradition. The American Negro's oral folk tradition took form in the plantation culture of the South and remained largely invisible during the period of slavery. (It is interesting to note that northern freedmen who settled in free states possessed none of the typical folk ways of the enslaved southern blacks.)[11]

While stressing the need to make use of the Negro's folk culture, Locke also, as a cultural pluralist, believed that Negroes would have to draw from both racial and national sources if they were to gain pluralistic equality. Early in his life Locke had observed that American Negroes, like other ethnic groups, had a tradition that they could contribute to America—a tradition worthy of being accepted on a par with any others. When returning from Europe in 1912, his first public speech was not on his European travels but on the need to develop this tradition.[12] Furthermore, the rediscovery of their rich tradition would not only open rich creative sources but would provide for Negroes a sense of racial continuity and equality. Recognition and acceptance of the Negro's cultural contributions would inspire other ethnic groups to rediscover their own traditions, he hoped, and this would serve as an example of the potentialities of cultural diversity and reciprocity. In this way, the cultural life of all Americans could be enriched.

10. Bernard Bell, *Folk Roots of Contemporary Afro-American Poetry* (Detroit: Broadside Press, 1974), 20–30. Bell states that there is "a lack of evidence that Locke, Johnson, or Du Bois had read Herder." However, I would assume that, as a philosopher, Locke had very likely read Herder's theories, as possibly had Du Bois and Johnson.

11. J. Mason Brewer, *American Negro Folklore* (New York: Quadrangle Press, New York Times, 1968), 86, 88; Richard Dorson, *American Folklore* (Chicago: University of Chicago Press, 1959), 166–68.

12. Holmes, "Alain Locke," 113–18.

The presumption of aesthetic value in folk art, or so-called high art derived from folk sources, may raise some questions for debate, but these questions are of more concern for those critics who tend to judge higher art as "pure." Those who favor folk culture as artistic material do not regard the two as being mutually exclusive, since both are concerned with the truth of human experience, folk art being a more direct expression of the people. Folk advocates attempt to deal with the problems raised by the traditional opposition between folk and formal art. The former is conceived to be childlike, primitive, and lacking in technique; the latter is defined as mature, civilized, and conscious of its art. There is, however, a consensus that the highest cultural values can be derived from what "cultivated" classes often refer to as the vulgar, lowest levels of society. These "lower layers" of society are not devoid of cultural significance; they are, in fact, a major source of materials that sophisticated society uses to fashion its literary expression. These original materials are acknowledged to be aesthetically valid on their own terms.[13]

Whether consciously or unconsciously influenced by Herderian theory or other philosophies of folk theory, Locke and other renaissance advocates of Negro culture were keenly aware of the value of folk culture and were in line with other adherents of folk sources. Locke was ultimately to write, "Folk expression raised to the level of conscious art provides much originality and beauty. That is the full promise of Negro art as the inner vision sees it."[14]

IV

While Negro folk material had been used in the late nineteenth century by Paul Lawrence Dunbar and Charles Chesnutt, the New Negro writers were the first to make more extensive use of this important body of folk songs and other folk material. Moving away from the dialect tradition, they created new forms based on the

13. Gene Bluestein, *The Voice of the Folk* (Amherst: University of Massachusetts Press, 1965), 7, 11.

14. Alain Locke, "Beauty Instead of Ashes," *Nation*, CXXVI (April 18, 1928), 432–34.

spirituals, blues, ballads, and work and dance songs, as well as the folk sermon. The most important and dedicated experimenter with these forms was the poet and writer Langston Hughes.[15]

Hughes began his literary career committed to the use of black folk and cultural material as one of the important bases of his art. Keenly aware of the Negro's position and condition in American society, he sought to translate the essence of the black experience, especially that of the urban, folksy Negro, into creative expression. Hughes showed by example and experiment the importance of the folk contribution to black writing through his use of the blues, spirituals, ballads, jazz, and folk speech. Being possessed of a great sense of personal freedom, an insight into the human condition, and an ability to identify with the "folk" permitted him to infuse his writing with a kind of humor and candor without the self-consciousness that frequently stifled other artists. Blues and jazz were the music of urban folk, and Hughes regarded jazz as one of the "inherent expressions of Negro life in America; the eternal tom-tom beating in the Negro soul—the tom-tom of revolt against weariness in a white world, a world of subway trains, and work, work, work; the tom-tom of joy and laughter, and pain swallowed in a smile." Hughes's use of blues forms and jazz rhythms was without doubt a major innovation of the Harlem Renaissance.[16]

Black culture, in Hughes's opinion, had a "great field of unused material ready for his art—sufficient matter to furnish a black artist with a lifetime of creative work, even among the better classes with their 'white culture' and conscious American manners, but still different enough to be Negro."[17] But it was for the "lower" classes that he had a special appreciation.

15. Davis, *From the Dark Tower*, 65.
16. George E. Kent, "Langston Hughes and Afro-American Folk and Cultural Tradition," in Thurman B. O'Daniel (ed.), *Langston Hughes: Black Genius* (New York: William Morrow, 1971), 183; George E. Kent, "Patterns of the Harlem Renaissance," in Arna Bontemps (ed.), *The Harlem Renaissance Remembered* (New York: Dodd, Mead, 1972), 40.
17. Langston Hughes, "The Negro Artist and the Racial Mountain," in Nathan Huggins (ed.), *Voices from the Harlem Renaissance* (New York: Oxford University Press, 1976), 306.

But then there are the low-down folks, the so-called common element, and they are the majority—may the Lord be praised! . . . Their joy runs, bang! into ecstasy. Their religion soars to a shout. Work a little maybe today, rest a little tomorrow. Play awhile. Sing awhile. O let's dance. These common people are not afraid of spirituals, as for a long time their more intellectual brethren were, and jazz is their child. They furnish a wealth of colorful, distinctive material for any artist because they still hold their own individuality in the face of American standardization. . . . And they accept what beauty is their own without question.[18]

Hughes's insistent use of "low-life" materials was the basis for disapproval from those who favored "best-foot-forward" and "race-uplift" portrayal of black life. This conflict served to underscore an apparent class bias that was at the root of much of the disagreement over how the Negro was to be depicted. The conflict existed between the middle-class or so-called genteel Negroes and their spokesmen, and the young and alienated who wanted to be free to define for themselves both the manner and mode of their artistic expression—to develop their own aesthetic. Another force at work, both subtly and overtly, was the expectations of whites with regard to the portrayal of Negro life. In his historic rebuttal to critic George Shuyler, Hughes said:

The Negro artist works against an undertow of sharp criticism from his own group and unintentional bribes from whites. "Oh be respectable, write about nice people, show how good we are," say the Negroes. "Be stereotypes, don't go too far, don't shatter our illusions about you, don't amuse us too seriously. We will pay you," say the whites. . . . The road for the serious black artist . . . who would produce a racial art is most certainly rocky and the mountain is high. . . . But we younger Negro artists who create now intend to express our individual dark-skinned selves without fear or shame. . . . We build our temples for tomorrow, strong as we know how, and we stand on top of the mountain, free within ourselves.[19]

18. *Ibid.*, 306.
19. *Ibid.*, 307, 309.

Another writer who drew heavily from the folk tradition was the elder statesman and spokesman for the New Negro movement, James Weldon Johnson. Johnson's writing career spanned a long period and ranged from his earlier usage of the Dunbar dialect tradition to a style more nearly like that of the younger Harlem writers. Unlike Locke, Johnson did not harp on the importance of searching for beauty or vague spiritual values. He defended vigorously the New Negroes' choice of low-life subject matter and thought that there was a great deal of snobbishness implied in referring to the less literate and less sophisticated class of Negroes as "lower." He said: "At least as literary material they are higher. They have greater dramatic and artistic potentialities for the writer than so-called higher classes." He felt that attempts by writers to use these people for subject matter helped to make them articulate, and he continued to advocate emphasis upon the black masses and the folklore derived from them well into the 1930s.[20]

Earlier, Johnson had been an important voice in supporting the artistic explorations of the Negro's folk heritage; he later became an important and innovative handler of folk material, notably reflected in his 1927 publication of God's Trombones. Considered to be Johnson's most brilliant and creative achievement of the Harlem Renaissance, God's Trombones is based on the sermons of black folk preachers.[21] Johnson imbued these sermons with sincerity, dignity, and eloquence. While they are free of dialect and far removed from the more comic effects of earlier treatments of this genre, Johnson used ungrammatical expression and added syllables for euphonic and rhythmic effect. The serious intent was never forgotten, and the result was genuine poetry. God's Trombones was a noteworthy achievement, and Johnson's success with the poetic use of the folk sermon, as well as spirituals, had considerable effect on later renaissance writers. Others added the ballad and the blues form, thus widening the range of folk expression.

20. Young, *Black Writers of the Thirties*, 149, 150.
21. Kent, "Patterns of the Harlem Renaissance," 44.

V

In the introduction to *The Negro and His Music*, Locke conjectured that "if American civilization had absorbed instead of exterminated the American Indian, his music would be the folk music of this country. . . . Full of the wind, woods and waters, the Indians' music was noble and simple, but interest in preserving it came too late. Thus it was to be the lot of Negroes to furnish for America its most distinctive and original folk music." This latter view was shared by Du Bois and others. Early American settlers generally relegated music to worship only, having a puritan bias against spontaneous song "as a child of sin and the devil, dangerous to work, seriousness, and moral restraint.[22] If mere hardship, hard work, and the rigors of the climate were the only reasons for the lack of a folk music tradition in colonial America, Locke contended, then the music of many folk groups could never be explained, particularly that of Russian peasants, for instance. Noting earlier this same barrenness of a folk tradition in America, Du Bois wrote in his essay on the sorrow songs in 1903: "Little of beauty has America given the world save the rude grandeur God himself stamped on her bosom; the human spirit in this new world has expressed itself in vigor and ingenuity rather than in beauty. And so by fateful chance the Negro folk-song—the rhythmic cry of the slave—stands today not simply as the sole American music, but the most beautiful expression of human experience born this side of the seas."[23]

Much of the folk heritage of the Negro was to be found in his music, and members of the Harlem movement led by Locke and Du Bois felt that spirituals and jazz in particular held great promise as material for artistic development. Locke described spirituals as "the most characteristic product of Negro genius to date," ranking them with the classic folk traditions of the world "because of their

22. Alain Locke, *The Negro and His Music* (New York: Arno Press and New York Times, 1969), 2.
23. W. E. B. Du Bois, "Of the Sorrow Songs," in *The Souls of Black Folks* (New York: New American Library, 1969), 265.

moving simplicity, their characteristic originality, and their universal appeal." Citing Anton Dvorak's use of spirituals as thematic material to represent the American atmosphere in his *Symphony from the New World* (1894), Locke felt that other composers would likewise eventually use spirituals as thematic materials in symphonic music or in larger choral forms. Indeed, Locke envisioned spirituals forming the basis for a tradition of American choral music similar to the great Russian choral tradition based on its folk music.[24]

Suggesting some justifiable ambivalence in what the use of spirituals and other folk music as the basis for composition could do to destroy the "folk atmosphere and epic spirituality" of this music, Locke recommended spirituals as the material for classical music, warning at the same time of "artificial compositions which imitate folk spirituals, or dress them up in sentimental and concert versions." He cautioned that "a genuine spiritual is always a folk composition or group product, spontaneously composed as a choral expression of religious feeling."[25] He agreed with Zora Neale Hurston, who described artificial derivatives of these songs as "Neo-Spirituals." She said that "these renovated spirituals are a valuable contribution to musical literature, but they are not the genuine thing."[26] While acknowledging the pitfalls, Locke nevertheless concluded that "spirituals are promising material for Negro music of the future, from which a great creative composer might develop a great liturgical music."[27]

Locke noted that a great folk music deserves and demands a great classical music. Although we are a musical people as evidenced by the great gift for spontaneous harmonization in song, Locke admonished that Negroes had as yet produced too few great musicians, especially in the ranks of composers. He observed that "our musicians with formal training are cut off from the people and the vital roots of folk music, and live uncreatively in the cloisters of the

24. Locke, *The Negro and His Music*, 20.
25. *Ibid.*, 21.
26. Zora Neale Hurston, "Spirituals and Neo-Spirituals," in Nancy Cunard (ed.), *Negro: An Anthology* (New York; Frederick Ungar, 1935), 359.
27. Locke, *The Negro and His Music*, 5.

conservatories, many of them under the palling taboos of musical respectability." Noting that many great schools of national music had once been in this retarded state, Locke took heart from the budding signs of serious music and hoped that composers—both Negro and white—would push forward a tradition of classical American music based on the rich lore of Negro folk music.[28]

VI

The collection and utilization of its folklore is an important means of documenting the history of any culture, and while others were urging the use of folk culture in creative expression, Arthur Huff Fauset was emphasizing the need to do scientific collection of this material. "Sentimental admonition and amateurish praise can never adequately preserve or interpret this precious material," he wrote. Fauset thought of folklore as documentary, and was convinced that much of what was the distinctively Negro character was to be found in his folk materials. He felt, however, that the main themes of folktales were intercultural. Compiling the materials of the southern Negro would give America some cultural texture and richness and would at the same time relate it to the vast and complex world literature. Fauset felt that Negro folklore was important for its intrinsic worth and for its comparative value. He felt that all great folk literature had several values that should be considered in its appraisal: 1) lack of self-conscious elements found in ordinary literature, 2) nearness to nature, and 3) universal appeal.[29]

Interest in the collection of folk material was to be the lasting contribution of Zora Hurston, one of the Harlem writers who was to utilize a full range of the folk culture. Like Hughes, Hurston was deeply committed to Negro folk life and culture because of its intrinsic value and interest. She maintained a lifelong interest in folklore, and as a writer and novelist she was perhaps at her best when she stuck closely to these themes. Trained in anthropology at Bar-

28. *Ibid.*, 5–6.
29. Arthur Huff Fauset, "American Folk Literature," in Locke (ed.), *The New Negro*, 238, 241, 242.

nard College and a student and protégée of Franz Boas, she did extensive collection of folklore in her native Florida, as well as in Alabama and Louisiana, and studied voodoo in Haiti. Her major contribution in the collection of folklore resides in her volume, *Mules and Men.* Gifted with a keen ear for voice sounds and rhythms, Hurston transcribed the speech of the common rural Negro and used this, together with his manner and superstitions, as the basis for much of her work. Hurston wrote: "Negro Folklore is not a thing of the past. It is still in the making. Its great variety shows the adaptability of the black man: nothing is too old or too new, domestic or foreign, high or low for his use."[30]

To use this great range of folklore creatively and artistically was a major aim of the New Negro movement. That many succeeded is a lasting contribution of the artists, musicians, and writers of the Harlem Renaissance.

---

30. Young, *Black Writers of the Thirties,* 219; Zora Neale Hurston, "Characteristics of Negro Expression," in Cunard (ed.), *Negro: An Anthology,* 27. For a thorough treatment of Hurston's life and career, see Robert E. Hemenway, *Zora Neale Hurston: A Literary Biography* (Urbana: University of Illinois Press, 1977).

Alain Locke and the Honest Propaganda of Truth and Beauty

GEORGE HALL

For Alain Locke, propaganda was the slanted rhetoric that he cautioned the Negro writers of the Harlem Renaissance to avoid. Being a Negro, he knew the harmful effects the contented slave stereotype of a Thomas Nelson Page, the buffoonery of an early Roark Bradford, and the savage beast in the works of Thomas Dixon had on his race. He knew that the works of these authors, aside from presenting such insulting and distorted images, neither had verisimilitude nor were they great literature. Difficult as it would be for a black writer to observe the world around him without wishing to cry out in rage at the injustices heaped daily on himself or his people, Locke cautioned a restraint and an attention to craft for black authors.

In 1925, Locke, the mentor to the young writers of the Harlem Renaissance, looked with optimism on the future. "The intelligent Negro of today is resolved not to make discrimination an extenuation for his shortcomings in performance, individual or collective; he is trying to hold himself at par, neither inflated by sentimental allowances nor depreciated by current social discounts. For this, he must know himself and be known for precisely what he is, and for that reason welcomes the new scientific rather than the old sentimental interest."[1] This was an extremely difficult position in the wake of discrimination, but the Negro writer was to adhere to the Socratic dictum and create despite the psychological and social persecutions inflicted on him. The purpose of this essay is to show that Alain Locke's ideal of a Negro literature of truth and beauty was in reality an honest propaganda stripped of its negative connotations. In this context, honest propaganda denotes any work of fiction with objectivity, sincerity, clarity, and balance.

This honest propaganda was discussed briefly by W. E. B. Du Bois in 1926, when he reflected upon Locke's New Negro:

> With one point alone do I differ with the editor. Mr. Locke has newly been seized with the idea that beauty rather than propaganda should be the object of negro literature and art. His book proves the falseness of this thesis. This is a book filled and bursting with propaganda, but it is for the most part beautifully done; and it is a grave question if ever in this world in any renaissance there can be a search for disembodied beauty which is not really a passionate effort to do something tangible, accompanied and illuminated and made holy by the vision of eternal beauty.[2]

In essense, both Locke and Du Bois agreed about what constituted good art. It was the function of art on which they did not agree. Du Bois doubted if one could really have a disembodied art or beauty; but Locke was not seeking for the Negro writer a disembodied beauty. He expected "tangible" results from the Negro knowing himself through his folk cultural experiences, particularly given the Negro's special circumstances as an American citizen within the wider American cultural tradition.

From the 1920s, during the heyday of the New Negro, to his death in 1954, Locke reviewed the works of young writers in his annual retrospective reviews of the literature of the Negro in Opportunity and Phylon. He realized that the literature of the young writers was becoming hackneyed; that is, he felt that the young

1. Alain Locke, "The New Negro," in Locke (ed.), The New Negro (New York: Arno Press, 1968), 8.
2. W. E. B. Du Bois, review of Alain Locke (ed.), The New Negro, in Crisis, XXXI (January, 1926), 141.

Negro writers, wooed by white patronage, were not developing their talents in the direction of great art but were promoting, in some instances, new versions of old stereotypes. Locke expressed relief when the stock market crash of 1929 ended the glorification and exploitation of the writers both by whites and by themselves in trading their art for sensationalism and exhibitionism.

In 1928, on the eve of the Great Depression, Locke wrote about the effects of negative propaganda on an audience: "Artistically it is one fundamental question for us today—art or propaganda . . . my chief objection to propaganda, apart from its besetting sin of monotony and disproportion, is that it perpetuates the position of group inferiority even in crying out against it. For it leaves and speaks under the shadow of a dominant majority whom it harangues, cajoles, threatens or supplicates. It is too extroverted for balance or poise or inner dignity and self-respect." Locke believed that propaganda caused the Negro writer to return to a negation of his own self-image. Reiterating his theme of the renaissance, Locke exhorted writers to strive for objectivity, to repress their personal bias or hatred and create a balanced work, free of negative propaganda and with a serious purpose. "Negro things may reasonably be a fad for others; for us they must be a religion. Beauty, however, is its best priest and psalms will be more effective than sermons."[3]

To the Negro writer this "religion" had always been an added burden, the burden of either writing what white publishers dictated or, many times, not publishing at all. Although the Negro artist had gained much recognition during the renaissance, the conditions of social prejudice and discrimination had not substantially changed in his daily struggle with the white world. Certainly, Locke tried to nurture and bring to bloom the young Negro writers of the renaissance, but he was also aware of the discrimination the Negro faced and urged the young writers to make great literature their protest and their propaganda.

There were works by writers of the renaissance which came

3. Alain Locke, "Art or Propaganda?" in Nathan Huggins (ed.), *Voices from the Harlem Renaissance* (New York: Oxford University Press, 1976), 312–13.

close to Locke's ideal of a positive propaganda: Jean Toomer's *Cane* (1923), Rudolph Fisher's *Walls of Jericho*, and much of the poetry of Countee Cullen, Langston Hughes, and Claude McKay. But many of these artists, Locke felt, had not written as objectively as they were capable of doing. Writing in a 1928 retrospective review, Locke reminded the Negro artist to get down and write—the fad was over. He saw this as "a time to discriminate between shoddy and wool-fairweather friends and their supporters, the stockbrokers, and the real productive talents." His remedy for the literary excesses of the renaissance was "an introspective calm; a spiritually poised approach, a deeply matured understanding, for no true and lasting expression of Negro life can come except from these more firmly established points of view."[4]

But some of course did not agree with Locke's approach, or what Allison Davis referred to satirically as "our Negro school of hearty and pure emotion," in his review of Du Bois' novel, *Dark Princess*. Locke in his own review had said of the novel, "It fails the acid test for propaganda while the author falls an artistic victim to his own propaganda ambushes."[5] Davis, deploring the "catch-word" *propaganda*, wrote of Du Bois' *Princess*: "He has spoken to both our spirits and our intellects. There have been both fire and light in him. Propaganda . . . is his case, the bringing to the people inspiration and energy ordinarily beyond their reach."[6] Davis went on to say that Du Bois may have had to sacrifice some artistry for the inspiration, which, of course, is the crux of the propaganda-truth-beauty role of the artist. The idea to be emphasized is that Locke believed that imagination and cultural advancement would come precisely because of, and not in spite of, a propaganda-free literature; that a work such as *Cane* and Langston Hughes's first novel, *Not Without Laughter* (1934), were both sincere presentations without special pleadings or negative propaganda. Although neither work escaped

4. Alain Locke, "1928: A Retrospective Review," *Opportunity*, VII (January, 1929), 8–9.
5. Allison Davis, review of W. E. B. Du Bois' *Dark Princess*, in *Crisis*, XXXV (October, 1928), 339; Locke, "1928: A Retrospective Review," 9.
6. Davis, review of Du Bois' *Dark Princess*, 339.

Locke's constructive criticism, he felt that each work had elements of truth and beauty. He wrote that *Cane* has "a phenomenally earthy 'universal particularity'. . . . Although the novel is Negro through and through, it is deeply and movingly human. . . . To wish for more than this is to ask that the transmitting quality of expert craftsmanship be combined with broad perspective or intuitive insight, one or the other." Of *Not Without Laughter* he wrote, "As it is, despite immaturity of narrative technique, this novel is one of the high water marks of the Negro's self depiction in prose."[7]

At the time, Negro literature turned away from what Locke referred to as the "exhibitionism" and "Romanticism" of the renaissance, to a social realism in the works of southern whites such as William March, Lillian Smith, Erskine Caldwell, and William Faulkner. Locke was encouraged that in Negro fiction, particularly Richard Wright's collection of short stories, *Uncle Tom's Children*, the promise of the renaissance was on its way to being fulfilled. He believed Negro fiction to be approaching the mainstream. He hoped for a universal art of the Negro writer, with racial themes but empty of false propaganda, and for much more than a reportorial realism or narrow proletarianism. It was never the schools of literature that Locke protested; for him, the question was the balanced treatment of situation, character, and theme. It remained a literary problem. If one wrote to achieve social justice, let him also do justice to his characterization; if the Negro had rid himself of old stereotypes, let him not repeat similar stereotypes in his own works. Balance was all.

Nevertheless, lest one believe that Locke preached a truth and beauty for Negro literature only, one must read his essay "Jingo, Counter Jingo and Us," in which he answers Benjamin Stolberg's article in *Nation* (October 23, 1928). Stolberg had used a review of Benjamin Brawley's *Negro Builders and Heroes* as a platform from which to cry out against minority jingo. Locke, as foe of all jingo-

7. Margaret Just Butcher, *The Negro in American Culture* (New York: Knopf, 1969), 184–85; Alain Locke "This Year of Grace," *Opportunity*, IX (February, 1931) 49.

ism and chauvinist prattle in fiction or nonfiction, called jingo a necessary evil as an antidote to the jingo of the white majority against minorities. His greatest fear was that the minorities would be infected with the majority disease. But Locke repeated his belief that "Good art is sound and honest propaganda, while obvious and dishonest propaganda is bad art."[8]

It must have been difficult for Locke continually to experience the social discrimination around him and to keep insisting that Negro fiction, if it were to become great, should thrust aside invective in favor of balance and poise. But he generally chose to leave the invective to the majority. His province was art, and only if invective could be incorporated adequately and fairly in the writer's work could it become honest propaganda and, consequently, good art. Ralph Ellison's novel *Invisible Man* was considered by Locke to be one of the truly significant novels of the twentieth century written by a Negro. In 1945, Ellison supported Locke's statement that honest propaganda was good art: "I recognize no dichotomy between art and protest. Dostoevski's *Notes From the Underground* is, among other things, a protest against the limitations of nineteenth century rationalism; *Don Quixote*; *Man's Fate*; *Oedipus Rex*; *The Trial*. All these embody protest even against the limitations of human life itself."[9]

Locke felt that the Negro artist would eventually, through a sensitive interpretation of his own folk roots and culture, move into the mainstream of American literature, as artists from other ethnic groups had done. Since the Harlem Renaissance, many white critics have judged the literature of Afro-Americans according to a double standard for artistic excellence. In many cases the works have been judged as great art on the basis of their being "raceless" rather than their value as works of art. The works, therefore, have been regarded as "Negro" literature rather than as literature of Afro-

8. Alain Locke, "Jingo, Counter-Jingo and Us," *Opportunity*, XVI (January, 1938), 8.
9. Ralph Ellison, "The Art of Fiction," *Paris Review*, VIII (Spring, 1945), 58, 70–71.

American artists. It matters little whether a literature of truth and beauty, which Locke advocated through the years, has been recognized on its merits by white critics. Even when such a novel as Ellison's *Invisible Man* was praised by white critics as one of the best novels of the twentieth century, it was extolled for its "racelessness." David Littlejohn, reviewing the book in his *Black on White*, epitomizes this double standard: "He [Ellison] achieves his extraordinary powers through objectivity, irony, distance. He works with symbol rather than with act. He is at least as much an artist as a Negro."[10]

Littlejohn's assessment is a major example of the double standard of judgment that Locke believed would eventually vanish. However well meaning Littlejohn's "as much an artist as a Negro," it implies that until Ellison wrote, only whites were artists, and what a happy surprise to discover that some Negroes can be artists as well. In the evaluation of other Negro authors of the 1960s, Littlejohn finds very few protest-free or raceless works. But no one has used racial symbolism, folk stories, the spirituals, and the whole American Negro cultural experience more than Ellison did in *Invisible Man*.[11]

The double standard that white academicians and other critics used in judging the fiction of Negroes has a dimension that Locke hoped would disappear. Locke wanted the writer to be judged individually on the merit of his art, and he trusted the "guardians" of the Anglo-American literary tradition to be fair. A fairness may or may not be present in many white American critics, but the Negro artist will probably continue to have his problems because of the peculiar preferences of critics who have not made a thorough study of the history, art, or folk culture of the Negro. Perhaps a narrow-minded emphasis on the values of Western culture, assumed to be the highest culture, and on the Afro-American as an inferior one is

10. David Littlejohn, *Black on White: A Critical Survey of Writing by American Negroes* (New York: Viking, 1969), 110.
11. George Kent, *Blackness and the Adventure of Western Culture* (Chicago: Third World Press, 1972), 153–55.

a reason for the critical double standards. Alain Locke understood this could be a problem, but in the late 1970s, he would probably react with surprise at the slow development of the consciousness of many white critics.

A lack of understanding and fairness toward the Afro-American writer is one of the reasons that young black artists began in the late 1960s developing the black aesthetic. They eschew the Western tradition of a white truth and beauty and demand that "literature be an aesthetic grounded in Afro-American culture. Many of these new critics insist that, to have value, black literature must contribute to the revolutionary cause of black liberation; not merely in polemics against white oppression but also in re-interpretation of the black experience. All the new critics agree that the literature should not be judged good or bad according to the tastes of Europeans, but according to its presentation of the styles and traditions stemming from African and Afro-American culture." [12]

The importance of the black aesthetic movement, as Darwin Turner perceives it, is that these younger writers are explaining theory, not merely commenting on practice, whereas in the past, Afro-American critics assumed that the desirable standards were those favored by the white establishment. [13] Whether or not those black writers such as John Killens, Larry Neal, Imamu Amiri Baraka, Nikki Giovanni, and others will continue to pursue the black aesthetic seems auspicious for American literature as a whole.

Locke would probably say that the black aesthetic, with its themes and symbols of Negro culture, had been with us in the renaissance. It was, but literature still was judged good art according to a white tradition, which included white tastes and prejudices. Now, the truth and beauty are black. Urging the Negro to write out of his experience, using his racial background and the American cultural tradition, Locke assumed that the literature would be accepted or rejected on the artist's individual merits. Many of the

12. Darwin T. Turner, "Afro-American Literary Critics," in Addison Gayle (ed.), *The Black Aesthetic* (New York: Doubleday Anchor, 1972), 71.
13. *Ibid.*, 72.

novels, stories, and poems of Negroes have found this fair evaluation and acceptance, but the big three are still Wright, Ellison, and Baldwin.

The civil rights movements of the fifties, sixties, and seventies; the deaths of Martin Luther King, John and Robert Kennedy; and the Vietnam War—all have occurred since Locke's death and have affected both black and white American writers alike. But unlike Locke, who continually directed the young black writers of the Harlem Renaissance and after to put aside bitterness and militant rhetoric and to produce art, not propaganda, the new black writers have been urged to channel their anger to the cause of black nationalism; to exploit their blackness in their work by demonstrating in their music, art, literature, and themselves that they rejected completely the white aesthetic and the so-called mainstream of American literature; to enhance new themes, symbolism, and imagery unique to their Afro-American experience. Consequently, the new black writers have not accomplished what Locke envisioned. Rather than being immersed in the mainstream, they have stuck to their roots in the rural South and in urban society, and in their music, literature and art. Although Locke's dream for the Afro-American did not materialize, much progress has been achieved. The experience of the Afro-American is unique in America's pluralistic society, and I believe that the Afro-American writer in particular will lose his vibrancy, style, and perhaps his integrity if he does not continue to eschew the mainstream and follow the black aesthetic.

In the meantime, white America has grown and I believe continues to grow in its appreciation of Afro-American culture. For the Afro-American writer to become immersed in the mainstream would create a blandness where there was previously a richness of Afro-American truth and beauty.

Alain Locke and the Sense
of the African Legacy

JAMES B. BARNES

In *The New Negro*, a varied group of essays, stories, poems, and pictures published in 1925, Alain Locke offered an initial and formal attempt at defining what he assumed to be a grand cultural metamorphosis for the Afro-American.[1] In the foreword to *The New Negro*, Locke announced as his aim the cultural and social documentation of the New Negro. He contended that he was witnessing a "fresh spiritual and cultural focusing" as well as "a renewed race-spirit that consciously and proudly sets itself apart."[2] Moreover, Locke maintained that the significant changes in the Afro-American stemmed from his release from the fictions of the past and a rediscovery of himself. The New Negro's task was to discover and define his culture, and this was precisely what Locke was attempting—the building of a race and defining of a culture.

If the concept of a distinctive racial and cultural contribution was valid, it would have to be found in the special experience of the race

1. Alain Locke (ed.), *The New Negro* (New York: Atheneum, 1970). For another analysis of the concept of the New Negro, see Nathan I. Huggins, *Harlem Renaissance* (New York: Oxford University Press, 1971), 52–83.
2. Richard A. Long, "Alain Locke: Cultural and Social Mentor," *Black World*, XX (November, 1970), 87–90, has proposed the term *ancestralism* to describe the totality of Locke's race-spirit concept, which was grounded in Locke's profound respect for the African past and for the folk spirit developed in the American South.

itself.[3] Therefore, the entire race had to be scrutinized for clues to such a distinct heritage. While folk materials and the expression of the common man had to be the essence of such a tradition, heritage also demanded a continuity with the past, the transit of culture. When Locke and other advocates of the New Negro searched for their origins or attempted to discuss racial culture, the question of Africa always arose. And thus Africa became an essential enigma in Locke's attempt to build a race and define a culture.[4]

Because Africa was such a large question for Afro-American intellectuals searching for racial identity and cultural heritage, it became very important to Locke's race-building and culture-defining efforts. From Locke's vantage, a reassessment of the African past was an integral component to his success. And so he consistently discussed various aspects of Africa in his writings and greatly encouraged its study. Undoubtedly, Locke was thoroughly elated when in 1929 he noted "the most significant of all recent developments: the new interest in Negro origins." He was convinced that if any one thing would lead to a permanent reevaluation of the Afro-American, it was what he perceived to be a thoroughgoing change of attitude that was becoming established about Africa and things African. What Locke had recognized was a sudden shift from the level of gross curiosity to that of intelligent, human comprehension of, and sympathy for, the literature about Africa. The intellectual father of the New Negro believed he was witnessing a revolutionary change, not only in interest but in point of view and approach. Optimistically, Locke felt that such a thoroughgoing transformation of opinion and approach, with its implicit cultural recognition of the Negro in his own intrinsic rights, eliminated the possibility of returning to previous viewpoints because of the resistance of

---

3. For a discussion of Locke's sociological orientation, as well as that of several of his more eminent contemporaries, such as Du Bois, E. Franklin Frazier, Kelly Miller, and Charles S. Johnson, and their impact upon the development of Locke's conceptualization of the New Negro, see S. P. Fullinwider, *The Mind and Mood of Black America: Twentieth-Century Thought* (Homewood, Ill.: Dorsey Press, 1969), 92–122.

4. Alain Locke, "The Legacy of the Ancestral Arts," in Locke (ed.), *The New Negro*, 254–67.

facts instead of "the mere fluid tide of sentiment." Locke saw the result of this reevaluation of the African past as a "vast new gain that can be counted upon as a new artistic and cultural foundation."[5]

Five years earlier, in 1924, Locke had stated a belief in the galvanizing effect that the sense of a cultural past could provide, and he felt that the intelligent presentation of African art would supply that effect. Although there was an ocean and ages of experience between the black men of the two continents, Locke maintained that African art was the Afro-American's legacy despite the fact that it was impossible for twentieth-century Afro-Americans to discover any unbroken cultural ties or correspondence between Afro-Americans and Africa. Locke believed the existence of African art revealed that black men were the craftsmen of a disciplined and classical art. Therefore, the Afro-American need not consider himself "a cultural foundling without his own inheritance." Afro-Americans could be freed from imitativeness and indebtedness to the white Western culture, and the knowledge of African arts should provide, to Locke's mind, encouragement for Afro-Americans to pursue the long-neglected styles of painting, sculpture, and decorative arts. By adopting this African inheritance, Afro-Americans could create new idioms that would become a source of further inspiration.[6]

It was much easier, however, to use the African artistic tradition as a means of giving racial quality to art than it was to interest Afro-Americans in Africa. As early as 1924, a year prior to *The New Negro*, Locke was publically chastising Afro-Americans for their current lack of interest in Africa and a past interest that had been sporadic, sentimental, and unpractical. The major reason for this most unfortunate apathy, according to Locke, was the lack of widespread factual information about Africa, and Locke claimed it should be the first duty of Afro-Americans to cultivate and diffuse among themselves the knowledge of the African past and present.[7]

5. Alain Locke, "1928: A Retrospective Review," *Opportunity*, VII (January, 1929), 8–11.
6. Alain Locke, "A Note on African Art," *Opportunity*, II (May, 1924), 134–38; Locke, "The Legacy of the Ancestral Arts," 254–67.
7. Alain Locke, "Apropros of Africa," *Opportunity*, II (February, 1924), 37–40, 58.

Apathy toward Africa was a recurring theme in Locke's writings. In 1936 he stated that the arts and antiquities were important for the true understanding of African life and that nothing was less known and more misunderstood by the average Afro-American. Three years later Locke wrote, "Even with all our scientific re-evaluation, all our 'New Negro' compensations, all our anti-Nordic polemics, a certain disrespect for Africa still persists widely." In 1948, and in reference to Du Bois' *The World and Africa*, Locke stated that what Du Bois had been saying for decades about the then crucial and strategic importance of Africa should be self-evident. However, Locke still perceived a "state approaching apathy on the part of too many American Negroes on this, to them, most vital of all subjects." Still, in 1953, the year before Locke's death, he was yearning for the time when the knowledge and transforming evaluations of the higher levels of African culture, which Locke called "indisputable evidence of qualities and culture traits comparable to the better known culture traditions of the whole human race," would filter down to the level of generally educated men and women, especially educated Afro-Americans.[8]

Locke held the Afro-American colleges somewhat responsible for the lack of widespread factual information about Africa and the apathy toward Africa among Afro-Americans. With the study of African art and archaeology having become reputable fields of scholarly endeavor, Locke felt in both a reproach and handicap that in 1924 there were no recognized Afro-American experts in these fields. As a result, he was highly critical of Afro-American colleges for being reluctant to develop special scholarship in these directions. Over one-quarter of a century later, Locke still expressed concern for the lack of lay and professional interest in African studies and comparative research, and he continued to criticize Afro-

8. Alain Locke, "Deep River: Deeper Sea, II," *Opportunity*, XIV (February, 1936), 42–43, 61; Alain Locke, "The Negro: 'New' or Newer: A Restrospective Review of the Literature of the Negro for 1938," *Opportunity*, XVII (February, 1939), 36–42; Alain Locke, "A Critical Retrospect of the Literature of the Negro for 1947," *Phylon*, IX (First Quarter, 1948), 3–12; Alain Locke, "From *Native Son* to *Invisible Man*: A Review of the Literature of the Negro for 1952," *Phylon* XIV (First Quarter, 1953), 34–44.

American colleges for doing very little to develop and encourage the study of Africa, because of their "unfortunate mental alienation and disinterest."[9]

Another important concern running through Locke's writings on Africa was his petition for sound scholarship. In Afro-American responses to Nordic jingoists, Locke in 1938 called for "a scientific, sanely directed counter-statement, and not another deluge of bigotry, hysteria and counter-prejudice. Not for moral reasons, but for effectiveness, let us be saner than our opponents. And let us welcome as champions only those who are scientifically convinced and convincing." A year later Locke was again petitioning for "clear-minded interpreters of Africa." A reiteration of these concerns came in 1949 when Locke wrote that "if our knowledge of things African is to be sound and profitable, it must be based on an interest and scholarship which has accuracy and authority beyond challenge."[10] Nothing else would satisfy the Rhodes scholar and Harvard Ph.D.

Despite his petition for scientific scholarship and his status as a leading and recognized interpreter of what he termed the African heritage or legacy, Locke was often as ambiguous and enigmatic in his terms of definition as was the theme he was endeavoring to define. In 1924 Locke used, for perhaps the first and only time in his published writings, an interesting and quizzical phrase—"the homing instinct"—when he wrote: "But eventually all peoples exhibit the homing instinct and turn back physically or mentally, hopefully and helpfully, to the land of their origin. And we American Negroes in this respect, will not be an exception." Africa was not only the enigma in the race-building and culture-defining process but also the target of the "homing instinct."[11]

Locke also used unscientific but interesting terminology when he

9. Locke, "Apropos of Africa," 38; Alain Locke, "Wisdom de Profundis: A Review of the Literature of the Negro, 1949; Part II—The Social Literature," Phylon, XI (Second Quarter, 1950), 171–75.

10. Alain Locke, "Jingo, Counter-Jingo and Us," Opportunity, XVI (February, 1938), 39–42; Locke, "The Negro: 'New' or Newer," 42; Alain Locke, "Dawn Patrol: A Review of the Literature of the Negro for 1948," Phylon, X (First Quarter, 1949), 5–14.

11. Locke, "Apropos of Africa," 37.

identified one of the distinctive elements in the cultural background of the Afro-American as the "primitive tropical heritage, however vague and clouded over that may be." One of these clouds Locke referred to was slavery. Not only was the Afro-American physically transplanted, he was abruptly truncated from his cultural roots. The loss of traditional language, compulsory change in habits, and placement in a strangely different civilization had reduced the Afro-American to "cultural zero." Thus "the rapid assimilation was complete and without reservation."[12] This was somewhat of a rephrasing of what Locke had written in 1925, when he observed that there was little evidence of any direct connection of the Afro-American with his past except in his remarkable carryover of the rhythmic gift.[13]

However, with the very next stroke of the pen Locke was writing such things as, "But even with the rude transplanting of slavery that uprooted the technical elements of his former culture, the American Negro brought over as an emotional inheritance a deep seated aesthetic endowment." Three years later, in 1928, Locke wrote, "And yet from the earliest efforts at crude self-expression, it was the African or racial temperament, creeping back in the overtones of his half-articulate speech and action, which gave his life and ways the characteristic qualities instinctively recognized as peculiarly and representatively his."[14]

Later, in 1936, Locke classified the Afro-Americans' chief musical gift as their "instinctive mastery of rhythm." The reason he gave for the Afro-Americans' excelling most races in the mastery of rhythm was their long and intimate contact with the original source of rhythm, the dance. Locke believed that in Africa, the element of rhythm had reached a peak of development "admittedly unsurpassed." This racial mastery of rhythm was the one characteris-

12. Alain Locke, "The American Negro," *Annals* of the American Academy of Political and Social Science, CXL (November, 1928), 1; Alain Locke, *Negro Art: Past and Present* (Washington, D.C.: Associates in Negro Folk Education, 1936), 2; Locke, "The American Negro," 1.

13. Locke, "The Legacy of the Ancestral Arts," 254.

14. *Ibid.*; Locke, "The American Negro," 1.

tic that seemed never to have been lost, "whatever else was," and it had made and kept the Afro-American a "musician by nature and a music-maker by instinct." Although slavery resulted in loss of customs, the erosion of native cultures, and forgetting of language and ritual, rhythm memories and rhythmic skill persisted. While Bojangles (Bill Robinson) was excellent vaudeville, if listened to with closed eyes, his performance became an almost symphonic composition of sounds. What the eye saw was the tawdry American convention; what Locke heard was the "priceless African heritage."[15]

Locke was probably the first American to write perceptively on African art. He stated that it would never be known and could not be estimated how much African skill was blotted out during slavery. However, he believed Afro-Americans retained some memory of beauty, "since by way of compensation, some obviously artistic urges flowed even with the peasant Negro toward the only channels of expression left open, those of song, graceful movement and poetic speech." Stripped of all else, the Afro-American's own body became his prime artistic instrument. So it was the environment that forced Afro-Americans away from the craft arts and their old ancestral skills to the emotional arts of song and dance. However, when a few Afro-Americans did receive contact with the skilled crafts, Locke believed their work evidenced some remaining "slumbering instinct" of the artisan.[16]

In spite of the "slumbering instinct," the Afro-American's artistry was completely reversed. Locke maintained that in America his taste, skill, and artistic interests were almost the opposite of the original African ones. In Africa the dominant arts were decorative and craft arts such as sculpture, metalworking, and weaving. In America, however, the Afro-American's main arts became song, dance, music, and later, poetry. The original African arts were technical, rigid, controlled, and disciplined; thus, characteristic African

15. Alain Locke, The Negro and His Music (1936; rpr. New York: Arno Press and New York Times, 1969), 14, 135, 139.
16. Locke, Negro Art, 3.

expression was sober, heavily conventionalized, and restrained. However, the Afro-American's main arts were "freely emotional, sentimental, and exuberant," so that even the emotional temper of the Afro-American represents a reversal of his African temperament. Those qualities that were thought to be "primitive" in the Afro-American, "his naive exuberance, his spontaneity, his sentimentalism," were not characteristically African and could not be explained as an ancestral heritage. Rather, they seemed to Locke to be the result of the Afro-American's "peculiar experience" in America and the emotional upheaval of their handicaps and their compensatory reactions. While he agreed that these traits may have become very characteristic, for Locke they represented the Afro-American's acquired, not original, nature.[17]

Locke was misled when he compared the character of Afro-Americans and Africans, as he relied too heavily on nineteenth-century thinking and theories of racial and ethnic personalities. He drew many of his conclusions from an analysis of African art, especially sculpture, a brief visit to Egypt (the only African country he ever visited), and the sober, dignified African visitors he encountered when they visited Howard University. Certainly his limited exposure to the African reality and his failure to observe African music and dance affected his judgments.

While Locke called for accurate and authoritative African scholarship, he found it difficult always to discuss, in these same terms, the significance of Africa to Afro-Americans and was reduced to a simple assertion of faith in a valuable African legacy and to the use of unscholarly and unscientific terms. Other Afro-American intellectuals were equally perplexed by the African heritage. Many seemed to know, or sense, that Africa should mean something to the race and that there should be some race memory that tied black men together. Ambiguity and doubt, however, left the question unresolved.

Locke strongly believed that Afro-Americans, as well as whites,

17 Locke, "The Legacy of the Ancestral Arts," 254.

must become aware of the immemorial African past and render it presently a living past. This memory was to be created by means of exploration and study. And so for years he encouraged artists, musicians, and others to study the African sources firsthand. Locke himself became an avid collector of Africana, wrote about the lost ancestral arts of Africa, and traced the influence of African art on European artists in the early twentieth century. Also, he came to know a great deal about African influences in Haiti and other Caribbean islands.

To rediscover their racial souls, Afro-Americans had to go back, at least mentally, to the African past. Locke's efforts to instill some sense of this African heritage in the younger poets, artists, and musicians bore some fruit (see the works of Toomer, Cullen, McKay, and Hughes). However, Afro-Americans in general tended to reject the term *Afro-American* because they perceived themselves to be penalized due to this African difference. The hyphen represented a bondage and not a resource or power. However, Afro-Americans were encouraged to turn this newfound cultural legacy into a releasing endowment. This is what Locke attempted to do for all Afro-Americans.

Alain Locke's Theory of the Origins and Nature of Jazz

RUSSELL J. LINNEMANN

In 1936 Alain Locke published his highly acclaimed *The Negro and His Music*, in which he discussed the history of black music in the United States and tried to establish aesthetic norms by which to evaluate it. In this book, which incorporated much of his earlier writing on the topic, he attempted to show that the musical heritage of blacks, from plantation shouts and spirituals down to blues and classical jazz, was one of the greatest cultural contributions the race had made to America. It was his fervent hope that it would one day be the basis for the great national music that he believed this country was destined to produce.

His study traces seven distinct periods in the history of black music. They are:

1. 1619–1830 The age of plantation shout and "breakdown"—a period characterized by African reminiscences and survivals
2. 1830–1850 The age of the sorrow songs—the classical folk period that includes the great folk songs and spirituals
3. 1850–1875 The first age of minstrelsy as epitomized by Stephen Foster and other sentimental writers of ballads
4. 1875–1895 The second age of minstrelsy, which is dominated by farce, buffoonery, "coon" songs, the folk blues, and the "buck and wing"

5. 1895–1918 The age of ragtime, which includes musical comedy and vaudeville performances

6. 1918–1926 The jazz age, which is dominated by the artificial blues, dance comedy, and the stomp

7. 1926–1936 The age of classical jazz, which is characterized by the dawn of classical Negro music[1]

Locke, who was a trained pianist and enjoyed playing Chopin, felt that such works as R. Nathaniel Dett's "Juba Dance" and William Dawson's "Negro Folk Symphony" were excellent examples of what he considered the proper direction toward which black music should head, namely, the creation of an authentic classical Negro music.

Although classical jazz was only in its infancy when he wrote his critique, he envisioned that its innovative, demanding style would be a major source of inspiration for the development of what he called "classical Negro music." Despite a very strong bias toward traditional forms of music, Locke had a wide range of appreciation that led to a broad understanding of a variety of genres. He felt that classical jazz had several major antecedents, including African carry-overs, spirituals, folk music, popular music, and ragtime, along with early jazz itself. Like Du Bois before him, Locke viewed the spirituals as the most characteristic product of the black folk genius, and he ranked them among the finest folk expressions in the whole world, by virtue of their moving simplicity.[2]

If the spirituals were the apex of folk art, Locke clearly saw the importance of another folk strain in the development of black music—to wit, the secular folksongs as epitomized by ballads, the blues, work songs, and prison songs. This music, which he described as being of black peasant origins, has had a direct bearing on the nature of popular music, ragtime, jazz, and hence classical jazz. He subdivided this secular music into six zones, each with its peculiar characteristics (including English, Irish, Latin, cowboy, and hill

1. Alain Locke, *The Negro and His Music* (1936; rpr. Arno Press and New York *Times*, 1969), 6, 11 .

2. *Ibid.*, 18.

ballad influences). He argued that modern jazz evolved from the lower Mississippi strain, which had the most deeply traditional blues forms.[3] This is in part, no doubt, because it is there that the musical traditions of the other cultures least impinged.

Locke contended that folk ballads such as "John Henry" and work songs of various sorts, with their elemental brands of humor, sorrow, despair, or anger, gave the blues their unique thematic content. What was particularly important, however, in the relationship of blues to jazz was not just the theme but the form, as well as the musical rhythm and harmony of the genre.

Traditional blues verses generally have three lines, the second being a repetition of the first while the last line concludes the mood of the verse and is often epigrammatic in nature. As Locke noted, the form is well suited to impromptu songs and lyrics, as the repetition in the second line gives emphasis, the opportunity for improvised variations with the chance to create an original final line, and the occasion to vary the rhythmic structure before returning to the original pattern of the composition. The reiteration in the second line is the original "break," the interval that affords the brief moment for improvised rhythm and tone changes from which modern jazz was created. Locke, who regarded W. C. Handy as the father of the blues and the one responsible for making the idiom popular, claimed, "From such simple swaddling clothes that terrific giant of modern popular music has grown."[4]

Existing coterminously with various strains of folk music in the last half of the nineteenth century was minstrelsy. Music was only a part of the repertoire of the minstrel and often not a very important one at that, as he generally relied heavily on dancing and comic antics. The art form originated on southern slave plantations, but as early as thirty years before the Civil War, white imitators, generally in blackface, had begun to perform in northern theaters. After the Civil War, there were many black minstrels and troupes, but what had originated as white men imitating black people had evolved

3. *Ibid.*, 31, 34.
4. *Ibid.*, 33.

into a genre in which black performers were mimicking the imitations of themselves.[5]

Locke felt that one of the early great, white minstrel songwriters, Stephen Foster, was deeply influenced by what Foster called "Negroid folk ballads" (watered-down versions of black melodies and lyrics made palatable for white audiences) and had roughly the same relationship to the Negro folk song that Joel Chandler Harris had to Negro folklore.[6] By far the greatest minstrel, however, was James Bland, a virtuoso banjo player and composer of hundreds of songs, including "In the Evening by the Moonlight" and "Carry Me Back to Ole Virginny." Musicians like Foster and Bland used minstrelsy to create a genuine national form of popular music, one that contained strong elements of the black folk tradition and thus helped to bring it squarely into the mainstream of American musical experience.

The second age of minstrelsy Locke charitably referred to as an age of brass. Minstrelsy became even more popular for white stage audiences, but it degenerated into a slapstick caricature of black folk types replete with "coon songs" and buffoonery. It is out of this period that the stereotype of the Negro as "an irresponsible, happy-go-lucky, wide-grinning, loud-laughing, shuffling, banjo-picking, dancing sort of being" emerged. So bleak was the picture that Locke was convinced that if it had not been for the herculean efforts of the Jubilee singers in rescuing the spirituals from near oblivion, genuine Negro music in the United States would have been extinguished.[7]

The Gilded Age was death to virtually every serious form of American musical culture. Philistinism knew so few bounds that Irish and Jewish folk types as well as other ones were debased. So complete was the process, Locke believed, that most black musical tastes became corrupted and that not until the jazz age did true Negro techniques of singing and playing reappear.[8] The bankruptcy

5. *Ibid.*, 45.
6. *Ibid.*, 47.
7. *Ibid.*, 52–54.
8. *Ibid.*, 54.

of the period, while pervasive, was not total, as the spirituals were still embraced by a small, serious music public. According to Locke, if anything positive came out of the poverty of late nineteenth-century minstrelsy, it was that the genre laid the groundwork for the rapid public acceptance of black musical comedy and ragtime, which, when fused with the folk secular tradition of the age, ultimately gave rise to jazz.

Modern black musical comedy had its origins in the early 1890s with the appearance of "Creole shows," which had both black and white performers, and the slow growth of black touring groups like Mahara's Minstrels, which featured W. C. Handy. Locke asserted that these two phenomena were to lead to Bob Cole, Rosamond Johnson, and Sisseretta Jones on one hand and Bessie Smith, Duke Ellington, and the Cotton Club on the other.[9] Both groups broke with the blackface tradition of minstrelsy, and for the first time in decades, honest music and dance, instead of buffoonery, was emphasized.

Of vital importance was the fact that these productions began to reach large white audiences and give opportunities for black songwriters and composers to flourish and mature as artists. Cole's "A Trip to Coon Town," Will Marion Cook's "Darktown Is Out Tonight," and his "Clorindy, the Origin of the Cake-Walk," which he wrote in collaboration with Paul Lawrence Dunbar, introduced white theatergoers to an upbeat tempo that grew out of older "coon songs." The explosive popularity of the new musicals whetted the financial appetite of Tin Pan Alley and spawned a host of white imitators and black collaborators. One of the most popular was Ernest Hogan, who wrote the very forgettable "All Coons Look Alike to Me," which was set to ragtime by Tin Pan Alley luminary Max Hoffman.[10]

The rapid tempo and eccentric rhythm that typified much of this show music became known as rag, and soon a substantial segment of America was captivated by its syncopated swing. The turn of the

9. *Ibid.*, 58–59.
10 *Ibid.*, 61.

twentieth century saw the rise of pure ragtime, with composers such as Scott Joplin and Kerry Mills (he wrote "Whistlin' Rufus"), and its culmination in the classic rag piece, Irving Berlin's "Alexander's Ragtime Band."[11] The reemergence of the cakewalk, a dance that lent itself nicely to rag music, combined with the aggressive salesmanship of Tin Pan Alley, pushed the music to an unparalleled popularity almost overnight. Thus it can be seen that the late minstrelsy period, despite its lack of intrinsic musical sophistication, played a key role in the evolution of jazz, insofar as it led to ragtime.

Band leaders like Ford Dabney, James Europe, Will Cook, and W. C. Handy gradually converted their ragtime bands into musically sophisticated organizations of the first order between 1905 and 1915. During this period, Cook formed his American Syncopated Orchestra, which was one of the first groups to play what is now regarded as symphonic jazz. At roughly the same time, Handy, who in his early years despised the blues, developed the "blue note" and began to experiment with the "improvised musical 'filling in' of the gap between the short measure of the blues and the longer eight-bar line, the break interval in the original folk form of the three-line blues."[12] What developed from this experiment were such sensational compositions as "The Memphis Blues," "Beale Street Blues," and the "Saint Louis Blues."

Handy, who was a very accomplished musician, replaced the traditional improvised blues of the Mississippi Delta, which were normally played by itinerant individuals or small groups without formal musical training, with a very sophisticated, musically literate orchestra, thus creating instrumental jazz. Locke maintained that this instrumental jazz emerged out of folk jazz and was an elaborate superstructure built upon the folk blues.[13] Handy's style deeply influenced the music of Europe and Cook, thus tending to fuse the traditions of syncopated orchestral music, which grew out of musical comedy, and ragtime with the Mississippi black blues form.

11. *Ibid.*, 62.
12. *Ibid.*, 77.
13. *Ibid.*, 78.

Locke was of the opinion that despite white influences, jazz was a uniquely black music. He said that the music contained an irregularity of interval, a tone quality, and a pace of rhythm that once had been a Negro secret and was still a Negro characteristic. Furthermore, it had a special mood and style that was inborn in the typical Negro.[14] He felt that, as jazz spread and became more cosmopolitan, it became less typically racial and that white musicians could play it too. This, in good part, he attributed to the universal appeal and expressiveness of the musical form. In essence, Locke claimed that modern jazz emerged from the totality of the black musical experience—African antecedents, spirituals, blues, other folk seculars, minstrelsy, Negro musical comedy, and ragtime, in combination with certain innate racial characteristics. In retrospect, his analysis of the origins of jazz is still basically sound, though his concern with racial characteristics makes his prose seem awkward to the contemporary reader.

Locke regarded the jazz that emerged in the decade following the end of World War I to be a highly sophisticated music form that put heavy demands on its capable players. Citing Louis Armstrong, Locke contended that to be a good swing player, "a musician must learn to read expertly and be just as able to play to score as any regular musician. Then he must never forget for one minute of his life that the true spirit of swing music lies in free playing. . . . He must try to originate and not imitate. . . . To be a real swing artist, he must be a composer as well as a player." Locke went on to add, "For the process of composing by group improvisation, the jazz musician must have a whole chain of musical expertness, a sure musical ear, an instinctive feeling for harmony, the courage and gift to improvise and interpolate, and a canny sense for the total effect."[15]

Almost as soon as the music appeared, Locke detected it moving in two radically different directions. On one hand revolutionary playing techniques on the trumpet and trombone led to the growth

14. Ibid., 72.
15. Ibid., 79.

of "hot jazz," which centered in Chicago, while the saxophone led to the growth of "sweet jazz," which was dominant in New York.[16] Since many New York musicians also played in Europe, it was the sweet jazz of the East Coast that first made substantial inroads on the continent. The initial jazz revolution was largely technical in nature and created the limitless possibilities for different patterns that would result from various instrumental harmonies.

Black jazzmen, according to Locke, explored the possibilities of the genre in greater depth in the 1920s. He pointed to white musicians like Bix Beiderbecke, Frank Teschemacher, and Gene Krupa, who remained firmly ensconced in the hot school while black musicians like Louis Armstrong, Coleman Hawkins, Fletcher Henderson, and Duke Ellington seemed to be able to shift at will from one school to the other. These black jazz greats could change moods and styles almost effortlessly, while their white counterparts seemed to raise barricades.[17]

Locke argued that jazz was something much more important than simply a new musical form; the nature of jazz itself he saw as a profound cultural statement. It was his conviction that the music "incorporated the typical American restlessness and unconventionality, embodied its revolt against the drabness of commonplace life, put pagan force behind the revolt against Puritan restraint, and finally became the Western World's life-saving flight from boredom and over-sophistication to the refuge of elemental emotion and primitive vigor."[18] This made the music far more than either an exercise in virtuosity or an antidote for the sorrow of black people in America. It was for that reason he believed the 1920s properly should be known as the Jazz Age.

While Locke was of the opinion that jazz had cultural overtones for America in general, he also contended that it was one reflection of black cultural development in particular. In this vein, it should be remembered that the Jazz Age is also the period of the Harlem Re-

16. *Ibid.*, 80–85.
17. *Ibid.*, 86.
18. *Ibid.*, 90.

naissance, an era of dazzling literary, artistic, and musical brilliance. Talking about younger black artists, Locke asserted that "they have shaken themselves free from the minstrel traditions and the fowling nets of dialect, and through acquiring ease and simplicity in serious expression, they have carried the folk-gift to the attitudes of art. There they seek and find art's intrinsic values and satisfactions— and if America were deaf, they would still sing." [19]

Whereas older generations tended to express themselves in cautious moralism and guarded idealism, trying to "be representative" or to "put the best foot forward," the younger artists had the tendency "to evolve from the racial substance something technically distinctive, something that as an idiom of style may become a contribution to the general resources of art." [20] Clearly, Locke was certain that with the emergence of jazz, such transfusions of racial idioms with very modern styles of expression had already taken place. When seen in that perspective, it is obvious that he placed the development of jazz in the forefront of American cultural life.

In his famous essay, "Negro Youth Speaks," Locke proclaimed that a younger generation of black artists had emerged, one that felt free to explore uncharted ground. They were not bound by the claims of the past or by the limits of their self-consciousness. No longer was the Negro mind so caught up in its own social dilemmas that it lacked a necessary frame of reference for true intellectual and cultural development. The cultured elite was now spiritually free enough to offer America significant contributions as the end result of an emancipating vision, and art must be ready to accept such gifts and, consequently, to reevalute the giver. [21]

The use of such terms as *moralism, free,* and *self-consciousness* by Locke was not accidental; they reflected his opinion of the nature of jazz. The spirit of freedom and the lack of self-consciousness that permitted the exploration or improvisation of various themes typ-

19. Alain Locke, "Negro Youth Speaks," in Locke (ed.), *The New Negro* (1925; rpr. New York: Arno Press, 1969), 48

20. *Ibid.*, 50–51.

21. *Ibid.*, 52–53.

ified the creative brilliance of Harlem Renaissance figures like Ellington, Armstrong, and Henderson and mirrored the psychological connection Locke saw between jazz and the nonmusical art forms of the period.

The question of morality arose because Locke contended that younger black artists had enjoyed the happy release from the hampering habit of setting artistic values with primary regard for moral effect. The result was a healthy realism that included a dynamic musical swing of cosmic emotion such as only the gifted pagans knew. He obviously felt there was an erotic side to jazz, a manifestation of the earthy expression in the original peasant paganism out of which it arose.[22] Locke tended to regard this primitive eroticism as healthy, but when it occurred in music that catered either to prurient interest per se or to commercial interests, he deemed it to be decadently neurotic.

Like virtually everyone else who wrote about jazz in the two decades after World War I, Locke attempted to connect what he perceived to be the erotic aspect of the music to the changing social, psychological, and sexual mores of the period. He differed, however, from most others in that he believed that those who condemned jazz as a form of sexual expression of modern hysteria were not entirely wide of the mark. He said that the jazz cult "has had a direct relationship to the free sexuality of this age. However, instead of blaming it on jazz, the vogue of jazz should be regarded as the symptom of a profound cultural unrest and change, first a reaction from Puritan repressions and then an escape from the tensions and monotonies of a machine-ridden, extroverted form of civilization."[23] Seen in this light, the impulses that led to the challenging of conventional morality of the period are directly related to the fundamental nature of jazz.

Music critic J. A. Rogers, a contributor to *The New Negro* who was influenced by Locke, echoed these sentiments by citing the great conductor, Leopold Stokowski:

22. *Ibid.*, 48, 52; Locke, *The Negro and His Music*, 87.
23. Locke, *The Negro and His Music*, 88.

Jazz has come to stay because it is an expression of the times, of the breathless, energetic, superactive times in which we are living, it is useless to fight against it. Already its new vigor, its new vitality is beginning to manifest itself. . . . The Negro musicians of America are playing a great part in this change. They have an open mind and unbiassed [sic] outlook. They are not hampered by conventions or traditions, and with their new ideas, their constant experiment, they are causing new blood to flow in the veins of music. The jazz players make their instruments do entirely new things, things finished musicians are taught to avoid. They are pathfinders into new realms.[24]

Reflecting Locke's conceptions of jazz, morality, and the ethos of the times, Rogers contended that, despite its informalities and its morally anarchic spirit, the music had a major societal function. "Jazz with its mocking disregard for formality is a leveller and makes for democracy. The jazz spirit, being primitive, demands more frankness and sincerity. Just as has already been done in art and music, so eventually in human relations and social manners, it will no doubt have the effect of putting more reality in life by taking some of the needless artificiality out . . . so the new spirit of joy and spontaneity may itself play the role of reformer."[25]

For Locke, the function and nature of jazz transcended its musical form. He viewed it as a cultural statement and a sociological phenomenon. In the foreword to *The New Negro*, he stated, "Whoever wishes to see the Negro in his essential traits, in the full perspectives of his achievement and possibilities, must seek the enlightenment of that self-portraiture which the present developments of Negro culture are offering."[26] Like Rogers, Locke was convinced that jazz, as well as other cultural advancements, had democratic overtones. He contended that the cultural recognition blacks win would be the key for reassessing and bettering race relations and establishing their contribution to American civilization. Even if racism continued to prevent the Negro from full initiation into

24. J. A. Rogers, "Jazz at Home," in Alain Locke (ed.), *The New Negro*, 221–22.
25. *Ibid.*, 223.
26. Alain Locke, Foreword, *ibid.*, ix.

American democracy, Locke claimed that the cultural explosion, of which jazz was a significant part, would represent a significant, spiritual "Coming of Age."[27]

Change and development are inherent in the nature of jazz, and Locke asserted that from 1926 to 1936, the year his *The Negro and His Music* was published, jazz emerged into a classical phase and with it came the dawn of classical Negro music. He felt that Dana Suesse's "Jazz Nocturne," Otto Sesana's "Negro Heaven," Constant Lambert's "Rio Grande," and Lamar Stringfield's "Parade" were beacons of a new style. Unlike George Gershwin's "Rhapsody in Blue" and Paul Whiteman's orchestral compositions, the work of the aforementioned composers represented genuine developments of the intimate motive idioms of jazz itself.[28] Thus for the first time, he maintained, jazz was close to a fusion with the classical musical traditions of Europe and the United States. He reserved his highest praise for William Dawson's "Negro Folk Symphony," which, while staged in the Negro folk tradition, was orchestrated in a highly unusual manner, thus combining a uniqueness of theme with form.

Of the great pure jazz musicians and composers of the period, Locke was most enamored with the talent of Duke Ellington, whom he regarded as the pioneer of super-jazz. He considered him the most likely artist to create the classical jazz toward which so many were striving, and argued that his style had passed though more phases and evolved more maturely than had any of his competitors.[29] Such works as "The Birmingham Breakdown," "Hot and Bothered," and "Mood Indigo" proved to be preludes for his later works of the type of classical jazz that Locke hoped would develop. Indeed, the musical legacy of this fantastic composer is so overpoweringly brilliant that he is generally recognized as the father of classical jazz.

27. Alain Locke, "The New Negro," *ibid.*, 15–16.
28. Locke, *The Negro and His Music*, 113.
29. Alain Locke, "Toward a Critique of Negro Music," *Opportunity*, XII (December, 1934), 366.

Perhaps the greatest strength of Locke's interpretation of the origin and nature of jazz is its eclecticism. Rather than merely providing a narrow technical description of the music, he attempted to show how it grew out of the black past and how it related to the social and cultural milieu of the contemporary scene. There is also a sense of tremendous intellectual daring in his position that jazz would reach the apex of its status as art music only when fused with folk music traditions, including not just blues and spirituals but African rhythm patterns.[30] It is that broad vision which still makes Locke on music so provocative and readable today.

30. Locke, *The Negro and His Music*, 130–31.

Alain Locke on Black Folk Music

PATRICIA LIGGINS HILL

Generally, Alain Locke is regarded as the outstanding black philosopher-educator who defined and brought into focus the New Negro movement, the Harlem Renaissance of the 1920s and early 1930s. As a music critic he is less known; yet, as one of the earliest and most significant black cultural critics in America, Locke has provided us with a scholarly, technical analysis of black folk music. Written over a span of fourteen years, the corpus of Locke's folk music criticism can be found in the following of his works: *The New Negro* (1925), "Toward a Critique of Negro Music," *Opportunity* (November–December, 1934), *The Negro and His Music* (1936), and "Negro Music Goes to Par," *Opportunity* (July, 1939).

Dominant throughout these works is Locke's concern for establishing the importance of black folk music to American culture as a whole. To accomplish his objective he relies on methods of argumentation such as deduction; concise definitions and descriptions of the folk musical idioms including the spirituals, jazz, and the blues; and historical details of these folk idioms.

In *The Negro and His Music*, Locke argues that black folk music is "the closest America has to a folk music."[1] He deduces that "if

---

1. Very little has been written on Locke as a music critic. Consequently, one must rely heavily on primary sources and the following three critical works for this study:

American civilization had absorbed instead of exterminated the American Indian, his [the American Indian's] music would be the folk music of this country." Instead, as Locke insists, the task of establishing a folk music "fell to the lot of the Negro, whom slavery domesticated . . . to lay the foundation for native American music." According to Locke, the importance of black folk music to American culture stems from "the weak musical heritage of the United States, which is mostly Anglo-Saxon in origin and which has a very plain musical taste." This weak heritage Locke correctly attributes to "a Puritan bias against music as a child of sin and the devil, dangerous to work, seriousness and moral restraint." Because of the restraints of the Puritan ethic, Locke argues that black folk music had to overcome "a double handicap, for both music and the Negro were generally despised." However, in spite of the Puritan prejudice against music, Locke insists that black folk music had "become one of the main sources of America's serious or classical music." As he maintains, "it is almost as important for the musical culture of America as it is for the spiritual life of the Negro."[2]

Locke's observation that black folk music has played an important spiritual function for the black American is accurate. It has served as a survival mechanism for the race. According to Bernard Bell, "The elemental nature of the Afro-American folk tradition is the distillation of the Black American's struggle to survive in an alien and hostile environment. . . . This is the reality behind Locke's observation that the Negroes of his day relied 'upon the race-gift as a vast spiritual endowment for which our best developments have come and must come.'" Out of the black American's humble origins, Locke maintains in *The New Negro*, emanates "an epic intensity and tragic profundity of emotional experience, for which the only historical analogy is the spiritual experience of the

Bernard Bell, "Folk Art and the Harlem Renaissance," *Phylon*, XXXVI (Spring, 1975), 155–63; Richard Long, "Alain Locke: Cultural and Social Mentor," *Black World*, XX (November, 1970), 87–90; and John Lovell, *Black Song: The Forge and the Flame* (New York: Collier-MacMillan, 1972).

2. Alain Locke, *The Negro and His Music* (Washington, D.C.: Associates in Negro Folk Education, 1936), 1, 2.

Jews and the only analogue, the Psalms." As Locke points out, since slavery, "it has been the lot of the Negro in the United States to be the peasant class, and thus, to furnish the musical sub-soil of our national music."[3]

Locke's most thorough and technical treatments are on the spirituals and jazz. He defines a "genuine spiritual" in *The Negro and His Music* as "always a folk composition or a group product, spontaneously composed as a choral expression of religious feeling." He draws upon Zora Neale Hurston's description of the spirituals as a composition sung "by a group bent on the expression of feelings and not on sound effects." Locke, then, rephrases this definition and calls the spirituals "congregational outbursts under the pressure of great religious emotion—choral improvisations on themes familiar to all participants." He describes them as "the classical folk expression in the world because of their moving simplicity, their characteristic originality, and their emotional appeal."[4]

John Lovell points out that Locke believed Christianity is the power motif behind the spirituals. According to Locke, the spirituals "are among the most genuine and outstanding expressions of Christian mood and feeling, fit musically and emotionally if not verbally of standing with the few Latin hymns, the handful of Gregorian tunes, and the rarest of German chorals as a not negligible element in the modicum of strictly religious music that the Christian centuries have produced." Locke thus indicates that, even though he considers the spirituals to be powerful emotional outpourings of "Christian mood and feeling," he has reservations about them as classical verbal expressions. However, he believes that their broken dialect and grammar "were invariably the results of an instinctive euphonic sense in following the requirements of the musical rhythm." In spite of this limitation, he considers the spirituals to be "the most characteristic product of Negro genius yet in America."[5]

3. Bell, "Folk Art and the Harlem Renaissance," 159; Alain Locke, "The Negro Spirituals," in Locke (ed.), *The New Negro* (New York: Albert and Charles Boni, 1925), 200; Locke, *The Negro and His Music*, 13.

4. Locke, *The Negro and His Music*, 18, 20, 22.

5. Lovell, *Black Song*, 502; Locke, "The Negro Spirituals," 199–201.

Furthermore, in both critical studies, "The Negro Spirituals" (in *The New Negro*) and "The Sorrow Songs: The Spirituals" (a chapter in *The Negro and His Music*), Locke hails those who have helped to advance the beauty and knowledge of the spirituals. He credits W. E. B. Du Bois for rediscovering and recognizing the beauty and importance of the spirituals, as expressed in Du Bois' "The Sorrow Songs" and Henry Krehbeil, who in *Afro-American Folk Songs* gives these songs their first serious, critical analysis. Locke praises the latter for giving a balanced account of the rhythmic elements of these songs, "regarding some as the African component in them and others as the influence of the religious hymn." At the same time, Locke scolds James Weldon Johnson for overstressing the harmonic element of black folk songs over the rhythmic element. "Weldon Johnson thinks the characteristic beauty of the folk song is harmonic, in distinction to the more purely rhythmic stress in the secular music of the Negro." He warns that "both in music settings and in the singing of the Negro [s]pirituals, this subtle balance of musical elements should be sought after and maintained."[6]

In addition, Locke credits several black musicians for spreading the knowledge of the spirituals. In this light, he hails the efforts of the Jubilee Singers and the university choirs of Hampton Institute, Atlanta University, Calhoun Colored School, and Tuskegee Institute. Similarly, he praises such outstanding singers as Roland Hayes and Marian Anderson. Locke insists that Hayes advanced the cause of the spirituals by his "subdued, ecstatic and spiritual refined" manner. In "Negro Music Goes to Par," Locke praises Anderson's genius and mastery of song, which he feels derived from "the purest strain of Negro folk music . . . she learned early from the Spirituals and the atmosphere of that spiritual view of life, how to feel with deep simplicity and reverence, how to project with completely impersonal and absorbed power."[7]

Locke's critical observations on the black spirituals are profound and far reaching. Richard A. Long, writing in 1970, maintains that

---

6. Locke, "The Negro Spirituals," 200; Locke, *The Negro and His Music*, 206.
7. Locke, "The Negro Spirituals," 202, 208; Alain Locke, "Negro Music Goes to Par," *Opportunity*, XVII (July, 1939), 200.

"Alain Locke gives evidence of his great sensitivity for and knowledge of music. His analytical observations on the spirituals were two generations ahead of any thinking on the subject and are still the most sensible things said in print that can be understood by a layman." Long attributes much of Locke's knowledge of the spirituals to his close associations with several of their noted arrangers, such as Harry T. Burleigh, Edward H. Boatner, Hall Johnson, John Wesley Work, and many others.[8]

Locke's critical analysis of jazz is also insightful. His knowledge of jazz music is demonstrated in three of his works, *The Negro and His Music*, "Toward a Critique of Negro Music," and "Negro Music Goes to Par." In *The Negro and His Music*, Locke defines and describes the idiom. He defines jazz as "the Negro folk idiom carried over to harmony and orchestration" and ragtime as "the Negro folk idiom in melody syncopated rhythm." He admits that elements of jazz and ragtime can be found in other parts of the world, such as in Germany in the classical music of Beethoven. However, he argues that both jazz and ragtime are distinctively black in that there is "a distinctive racial intensity of mood and a peculiar style of technical performance that can be imitated . . . but of which the original pattern was Negro." Equally as important, Locke disputes the notion that the Paul Whiteman concert of 1924 is the official birthday of jazz. Instead, he insists that the Carnegie concert of 1912 is "truly 'the birthday of jazz', while the Whiteman concert is 'the coming of age party' for jazz."[9]

In "Toward A Critique of Negro Music" Locke exhibits a pessimism that stems from his perception that black folk music, particularly jazz, has become diluted because of its enslavement to poor critical analysis and the commercialism of Tin Pan Alley. He rates most of black folk music criticism as "platitudinous piffle—repetitious bosh; the pounds of praise being, if anything, more hurtful and damning than the ounces of disparagement." The black folk musicians are, he continues, "in commercial slavery to Tin Pan

8. Long, "Alain Locke," 89.
9. Locke, *The Negro and His Music*, 70, 72.

Alley and subject to the corruption and tyranny of the ready cash of our dance halls and the vaudeville stage."[10]

Locke is especially annoyed with the uncritical appraisal of jazz music. Particularly irritating to him is George Gershwin's approach to jazz. Gershwin says: "Jazz, I regard as an American folk music; not the only one, but a very powerful one which is probably in the blood and feeling of the American people more than any other style of folk-music. I believe that it can be made the basis of serious symphony works of lasting value in the hands of a composer with talent for both jazz and symphonic music." Locke has serious reservations about Gershwin's understanding of the functional relationship between art music and folk music. He argues that "only true genius and almost consecrated devotion can properly fuse art-music and folk music. . . . I question, very seriously, his [Gershwin's] easygoing formula of superimposing one [art music] upon the other [folk music]." He also criticizes Gershwin for not recognizing the "Negro idioms from which it [jazz] has been derived." In addition, he attacks Henry Cowell for saying so little on the subject of jazz in his book *American Composers on American Music*. Locke admits that "disappointment at what could have been said in this volume sent me into a turtle shell of silence." Furthermore, he is disappointed to find "the best criticism of jazz coming from foreign critics like Schwerké and Goffin."[11]

Last of all, while Locke praises such white composers as Aaron Copeland, Alden Carpenter, and Paul Whiteman for their pioneering use of jazz idioms, he scorns black musicians in general for not recognizing "the genuine values of Negro music." He does, however, credit Duke Ellington for his pioneer role and his mastery of the jazz music idiom. He lauds Ellington for "emancipating American popular music from text for the first time since Colonial days." "Within an Ellington composition," Locke contends, "there is a sim-

10. Lovell, *Black Song*, 502; Alain Locke, "Toward A Critique of Negro Music," *Opportunity*, XII (November, 1934), 328; Locke, *The Negro and His Music*, 328.
11. Locke, *The Negro and His Music*, 329–31.

ilar unity of style of the essential musical qualities of melody, rhythm, harmony, color and form."[12]

The future of jazz and black folk music as a whole looks brighter to Locke, however, in "Negro Music Goes to Par." He is encouraged because in the year 1939, black folk music, "instead of being sentimentalized extravagantly . . . is now being intellectualized seriously, soberly." Locke attributes this scholarly analysis of black music as the reaction of the swing era to the commercialization of the Tin Pan Alley period. He declares that "just as the Swing era has marked something of a reaction from the dilution and commercialization of the Tin Pan Alley period, so now, the faddist interest in Negro music is deepening into technical analysis." Locke is especially impressed with objective, technical analyses of jazz. In this regard, he considers Winthrop Sargeant's *Jazz: Hot and Hybrid* to be "the best and most scholarly analysis of jazz and Negro folk music to date. . . . The Negro sources are freely admitted and correctly traced, the important basic denominators of idioms common to the Negro's religious and secular folk music are clearly seen, the periods of development are competently sketched with the possible exception of the post–Civil War period, where there is little documentation anyway; and most important of all, the musical idioms of modern jazz are carefully analyzed." Locke also agrees with Sargeant's perceptions that jazz rhythms, with polyrhythms and group improvisations as their primary characteristic, are "basically Negro, so much as to be in all probability derivative from Africa." Locke is particularly in agreement with Sargeant's chapter, "The Geography of Jazz Rhythm," which "admits characteristic differences between European syncopation and polyrhythm and dominant African and Afro-American varieties." He considers the chapter to be "a sensible solution of a vexatious controversial problem." Also, he praises Benny Goodman and his book *The Kingdom of Swing*. He regards Goodman as "one of the great constructive forces in the jazz world" and his book as "a documentation between

12. *Ibid.*, 329, 366; Locke, "Toward A Critique of Negro Music," 366.

the interchange of white and black musicians." Locke is, however, less impressed with Wilder Hobson's work, *American Jazz Music*, which he considers to be "more of a jazz fanbook, less of an objective analysis or survey."[13]

The body of Locke's jazz criticism is an intricate blend of textual analysis and creative thought. He carefully scrutinizes the views of various critics, composers, and musicians and simultaneously interjects his own creative thinking. He is most creative in his discussion of Sargeant's *Jazz: Hot and Hybrid*. Locke's recognition of the dominant African and Afro-American influences on, and elements in, black jazz is especially noteworthy. Such reliable contemporary critical studies as Ernest Borneman's "The Roots of Jazz," LeRoi Jones's (Imamu Amiri Baraka's) *Black Music* and *Blues People*, Kwabena Nketia's *The Music of Africa*, and Printz Walton's *Music: Black, White and Blue* support Locke's critical observations.

In comparison with Locke's treatment of jazz and the spirituals, his study of the blues has limited scope and lacks critical depth. The only discussion on the blues is found in his *The Negro and His Music*. In addition, in this work, Locke's definition of the blues as "a one-man affair originating, typically, as the expression of a single singer's feelings" is not accurate. The blues represents collective yearnings and feelings; the personal life of the blues singer becomes the prototype of the collective. According to Sterling Brown and Arthur P. Davis, in *The Negro Caravan* (1941), the blues singer is able to transmit a collective consciousness affectively, because the blues idiom is familiar to his or her audience. "In contrast to the spirituals, which were originally intended for group singing, the blues are sung by a single person. They express his feelings and ideas about his experience, but they do this so fundamentally, in an idiom [so] recognizable to his audience, that this emotion is shared as theirs." Jahnheinz Jahn goes further in his analysis of the blues as a communal art form. In "Residual African Elements in the Blues," he maintains that "[The Negro] does not in fact express his personal

13. Locke, *The Negro and His Music*, 196–97, 198, 199.

experiences and transfer them to his audience; on the contrary, it is the experiences of the community that he is expressing, making himself the spokesman."[14]

Notwithstanding, Locke is correct in his technical analysis of the blues idiom. He recognizes that "tunes are built around a succession of three common chords on the keynote, the sub-dominant and the chord of the dominant seventh." He also instructs us that the blues form "is admirably adapted to impromptu songs and impromptu versifying." He points out that the second line, the blues break, and the blue note give chance for emphasis and for improvisation. Notably, he recognizes that "the break is the narrow cradle for the improvised rhythm and eccentric tone intervals from which jazz was born." However, Locke does not give adequate consideration to the "cry" and the "holler," which Marshall Stearns, in *The Story of Jazz* (1958), considers to be one of the most important elements of the blues. "With the exception of the rhythm, perhaps the most important single element in the blues is the cry and holler . . . it is part and parcel of the blue note and blue tonality. In the cry, we have the ever-changing pitch in the melody of the blues." Locke does, however, recognize the significance of the blues. He maintains that it is "second only to the spirituals" as a black folk art form. He explains that, because the blues is "a secular or non-religious music of Negro peasant origin, for generations it was neglected and despised." In addition, he gives a brief historical sketch of the development of the blues. In this regard, he hails W. C. Handy, the composer of the "Memphis Blues," to be the father of the blues and gives a brief biographical sketch of him. He also mentions the talent of Bessie Smith and her composition "Gulf Coast Blues."[15]

In spite of Locke's limited and sketchy discussion on the blues, his studies on black folk music as a whole deserve serious critical

14. *Ibid.*, 32; Sterling A. Brown and Arthur P. Davis, *The Negro Caravan* (New York: Dryden Press, 1941), 426; Janheinz Jahn, "Residual African Elements in the Blues," in Alan Dundes (ed.), *Mother Wit from the Laughing Barrel: Readings in the Interpretation of Afro-American Folklore* (Englewood Cliffs: Prentice-Hall, 1973), 101.
15. Marshall Stearns, *The Story of Jazz* (New York: Mentor, 1958), 74; Locke, *The Negro and His Music*, 32, 33, 76.

attention. In essence, in black music criticism, Locke picks up where W. E. B. Du Bois and James Weldon Johnson leave off. While Du Bois, Johnson, and Locke all have made significant contributions in advancing the knowledge and importance of the black spirituals, Locke has gone even further in advancing the cause of black folk music in general. His recognition of black folk music as a serious and necessary art form and his dedication and critical abilities which have helped to establish it as such are quite evident. Essentially, what black folk music is to American music, Locke is to American music criticism. Just as the spirituals, blues and jazz, as Locke maintains, constitute the basis for American music culture, Locke lays a sound foundation upon which much of the serious, modern black folk music criticism is based.

Selected Bibliography
of the Works of Alain Locke

Books and Parts of Books

"Art or Propaganda?" In *Voices from the Harlem Renaissance*, edited by Nathan Huggins. New York: Oxford University Press, 1976.

"Cultural Relativism and Ideological Peace." In *Approaches to World Peace*. New York: Fourth Symposium of the Conference on Science, Philosophy, and Religion, 1944, pp. 609–18.

"The Legacy of the Ancestral Arts." See *The New Negro*, 254–67.

"The Need for a New Organon in Education." In *Goals for American Education*. New York: Ninth Symposium of the Conference on Science, Philosophy, and Religion, 1950, pp. 201–12.

The Negro and His Music. Originally published in 1936. New York: Arno Press and New York *Times*, 1969.

Negro Art: Past and Present. Originally published in 1936. New York: Arno Press, 1969.

"The Negro Group." In *Group Relations and Group Antagonisms*, edited by R. M. MacIver. New York: Institute for Religious Studies, 1944, pp. 43–59.

"The Negro Spirituals." See *The New Negro*, 199–213.

"Negro Youth Speaks." See *The New Negro*, 47–53.

"Negroes (American)." *Britannica Book of the Year 1940*, pp. 485–86.

The New Negro. Originally published in 1925, with numerous reprints. New York: Atheneum, 1977.

"Our Little Renaissance." In *Ebony and Topaz*, edited by Charles S.

Johnson. New York: Association for the Study of Negro Life and History, 1927, pp. 117–18.

"Pluralism and Ideological Peace." In *Freedom and Experience*, edited by Sidney Hook and Milton R. Konvitz. Ithaca: Cornell University Press, 1947, pp. 63–69.

"Pluralism and Intellectual Democracy." In *Second Symposium*. New York: Conference on Science, Philosophy, and Religion, 1942, pp. 196–209.

"Values and Imperatives." In *American Philosophy, Today and Tomorrow*, edited by Horace Meyer Kallen and Sidney Hook. New York: Lee Furman, 1935, pp. 313–33.

When Peoples Meet, edited with Bernard Stern. New York: Progressive Education Association, 1942.

Articles and Book Reviews

"The American Negro." *Annals* of the American Academy of Political and Social Science, CXL (November, 1928).

"Apropos of Africa." *Opportunity*, II (February, 1924), 37–40, 58.

"As Others See Us." *Opportunity*, II (April, 1924), 109–10.

"Beauty Instead of Ashes." *Nation*, CXXVI (April 18, 1928), 432–34.

"Black Truth and Black Beauty." *Opportunity*, XI (January, 1933), 14–18.

"The Boxed Compass of Our Race Relations." *Southern Workman*, LVIII (February, 1929), 49–56.

"The Command of the Spirit." *Southern Workman*, LIV (July, 1925), 295–99.

"The Concept of Race as Applied to Social Culture." *Howard Review*, I (June, 1924), 290–99.

"The Contribution of Race to Culture." *Student World* (1950), 349–53; copy in Trevor Arnett Library, Alain Locke Folder, Atlanta University.

"A Contribution to American Culture." *Opportunity*, XXIII (Fall, 1945), 192–93, 238.

"A Critical Retrospect of the Literature of the Negro for 1947." *Phylon*, IX (First Quarter, 1948), 3–12.

"Dawn Patrol: A Review of the Literature of the Negro for 1948." *Phylon*, X (First Quarter, 1949), 5–15.

"Deep River: Deeper Sea, I." *Opportunity*, XIV (January, 1936), 6–10.

"Deep River: Deeper Sea, II." *Opportunity*, XIV (February, 1936), 42–43, 61.

"The Dilemma of Segregation." *Journal of Negro Education*, IV (July, 1935), 406–11.

"Dry Fields and Green Pastures, II." *Opportunity*, XVIII (February, 1940), 40–46.

"The Eleventh Hour of Nordicism, I." *Opportunity*, XIII (January, 1935), 8–12.

"The Eleventh Hour of Nordicism, II." *Opportunity*, XIII (February, 1935), 46–48, 59.

"From *Native Son* to *Invisible Man*: A Review of the Literature of the Negro for 1952." *Phylon*, XIV (First Quarter, 1953), 34–44.

"Goat Alley," a review of Ernest Howard Culbertson's *Goat Alley: A Tragedy of Negro Life*. *Opportunity*, I (February, 1923), 30.

"God Save Reality! II." *Opportunity*, XV (February, 1937), 40–44.

"The High Cost of Prejudice." *Forum*, LXXVIII (December, 1927), 500–10.

"The High Price of Integration." *Phylon*, XIII (First Quarter, 1952), 7–18.

"Jingo, Counter-Jingo and Us." *Opportunity*, XVI (January, 1938), 7–11, 27, and XVI (February, 1938), 39–42.

"Minorities and the Social Mind." *Progressive Education*, XIII (March, 1935), 141–46.

"Negro Music Goes to Par." *Opportunity*, XVII (July, 1939), 196–200.

"The Negro: 'New' or Newer: A Retrospective Review of the Literature of the Negro for 1938." *Opportunity*, XVII (February, 1939), 36–42.

"The Negro Speaks for Himself." *Survey*, LII (April 15, 1924), 71–72.

"The Negro's Contribution to American Culture." *Journal of Negro Education*, VIII (July, 1939), 521–29.

"1928: A Retrospective Review." *Opportunity*, VII (January, 1929), 8–11.

"A Notable Conference." *Opportunity*, VIII (May, 1930), 137–40.

"A Note on African Art." *Opportunity*, II (May, 1924), 134–38.

"The Role of the Talented Tenth." *Howard University Record*, XII (December, 1918), 15–18.

"This Year of Grace." *Opportunity*, IX (February, 1931), 48–51.

"Toward A Critique of Negro Music." *Opportunity*, XII (November, 1934), 365–67, 385, and XII (December, 1934), 328–31.

"Unity Through Diversity: A Baha'i Principle." *Baha'i World*, IV (1930), 372–74.

"Values That Matter." *Key Reporter*, XIX (May, 1954).
"We Turn To Prose." *Opportunity*, X (February, 1932), 40–44.
"Welcome the New South—A Review." *Opportunity*, IV (December, 1926), 374–75.
"Whither Race Relations? A Critical Commentary." *Journal of Negro Education*, XIII (Summer, 1944), 398–406.
"Wisdom de Profundis: Review of the Literature of the Negro, 1949; Part II—The Social Literature." *Phylon*, XI (Second Quarter, 1950), 171–75.
"The Younger Literary Movement," written with W. E. B. Du Bois. *Crisis*, XXVII (February, 1924), 161–63.

Miscellaneous

See Aptheker, Herbert, ed. *The Correspondence of W. E. B. Du Bois.* 2 vols. Amherst: University of Massachusetts Press, 1973, 1976.
"The Problem of Classification in the Theory of Value." Ph.D. dissertation, Harvard University, 1918.

who is Black?

Notes on Contributors

JAMES B. BARNES is chairman of the Division of Continuing Education at Marion College and is also an associate professor of education. He earned his Ed.S. from George Peabody College and his Ed.D. from the University of Georgia. In 1971 he won a grant to attend the Afro-American Studies Institute at Kentucky State College. He has written *A Black Studies Film Seminar: A Study of Racial Attitudes.*

A. GILBERT BELLES is associate professor of history at Western Illinois University, where he currently teaches a wide variety of courses in black history. He earned his Ph.D. from Vanderbilt University and has received several awards from the National Endowment for the Humanities. He is currently completing a monograph on the Harlem Renaissance.

REBECCA T. CUREAU, associate professor of music at Southern University, is the director of the Women's Ensemble and teaches courses in piano and music theory. She earned her M.Mus. from Northwestern University and has done additional study at several schools including the University of Michigan and Louisiana State University. She is currently listed in the *International Who's Who of Women in Education.*

RUTLEDGE M. DENNIS, associate professor of sociology at Virginia Commonwealth University, earned his Ph.D. from Washington State University. He has published articles on prejudice and discrimination, W. E. B. Du Bois, the sociology of sociology, and the sociology of intellectuals. He has contributed, along with Charles Jarmon, to *Afro-Americans: A Social Science Perspective* and is currently working on a case study of urban annexation.

GEORGE HALL is associate professor of English at the University of Maine at Presque Isle. He is currently on a leave of absence and is teaching at Saint Anselm's College. He earned his Ph.D. from the University of Utah and is primarily interested in Afro-American literature, the eighteenth-century novel, and Elizabethan studies. He has also done work on the scope of Locke's literary criticism.

WILLIAM B. HARVEY is director of the Advancement on Individual Merit Program at the State University of New York at Stony Brook and also teaches there in the African Studies Program. He did his doctoral work at Rutgers University on the anthropology of education and was formerly associate dean of students and assistant professor of education at Earlham College. He is a former journalist and is working on a book about education in the Third World.

PATRICIA L. HILL is associate professor of English and ethnic studies at the University of San Francisco and is also director of ethnic studies there. She is an honors graduate from Howard University and earned her Ph.D. from Stanford University. She is an article and book reviewer for the *San Francisco Review of Books* and the *Western Journal of Black Studies* and is presently writing a book on the aesthetics of the Third World.

RUSSELL J. LINNEMANN is associate professor of history at the University of Tennessee at Chattanooga. He earned his Ph.D. from the University of Michigan and is interested mainly in African history and literature, Afro-American studies, and British Empire history. He has published several articles and reviews. He has won three National Endowment for the Humanities awards, three grants from the UC Foundation, and was named to a State Department fellowship. He is currently working on a book, *British Literary Images of Africa in the Nineteenth and Twentieth Centuries*.

MANNING MARABLE, associate professor of history at Cornell University, has taught at both Tuskegee Institute and the University of San Francisco. He is preparing a history of Tuskegee. The focus of his interest in Afro-American studies is the life and work of W. E. B. Du Bois, and he is also doing research in Marxist studies.

ERNEST D. MASON is associate professor of English and director of the University Honors Center at North Carolina Central University. He earned his Ph.D. from Emory University in philosophy and interdisciplinary studies He is principally interested in Afro-American studies, value theory, aesthetics, and hermeneutics. He has published articles in *Obsidian* and *Baha'i World* and is currently working on a book about the philosophical dimension of autobiography as well as several articles.

Index